P9-CCP-338

ESSENTIAL GUIDE TO
E

46367

KF
590
.Z9
W368
2001

Warda, Mark.
    Essential guide to real estate
leases: with forms /

DATE DUE

LIBRARY
SOUTHWEST WI TECHNICAL COLLEGE
1800 BRONSON BLVD
FENNIMORE, WI 53809

ESSENTIAL GUIDE TO REAL ESTATE LEASES

Knox Learning Center
SW Tech Library Services
1800 Bronson Boulevard
Fennimore, WI 53809

Mark Warda
Attorney at Law

SPHINX® PUBLISHING
AN IMPRINT OF SOURCEBOOKS, INC.®
NAPERVILLE, ILLINOIS

Copyright © 2001 by Mark Warda
Cover design © 2001 by Sourcebooks, Inc.®

All rights reserved. No part of this book may be reproduced in any form or by any electronic or mechanical means including information storage and retrieval systems—except in the case of brief quotations embodied in critical articles or reviews, or in the case of the exercises in this book solely for the personal use of the purchaser—without permission in writing from its publisher, Sourcebooks, Inc.®
This book was formerly titled *How to Negotiate Real Estate Leases*. We have updated or changed the forms, statutes, and information in addition to changing the title to ensure that it is the most current as of the time of publication.

First Edition, 2001
Published by: **Sphinx® Publishing, An Imprint of Sourcebooks, Inc.®**

<u>Naperville Office</u>
P.O. Box 4410
Naperville, Illinois 60567-4410
630-961-3900
Fax: 630-961-2168
http://www.sourcebooks.com

This publication is designed to provide accurate and authoritative information in regard to the subject matter covered. It is sold with the understanding that the publisher is not engaged in rendering legal, accounting, or other professional service. If legal advice or other expert assistance is required, the services of a competent professional person should be sought.
From a Declaration of Principles Jointly Adopted by a Committee of the American Bar Association and a Committee of Publishers and Associations

This product is not a substitute for legal advice.

Disclaimer required by Texas statutes.

Library of Congress Cataloging-in-Publication Data
Warda, Mark.
    Essential guide to real estate leases : with forms / Mark Warda.-- 1st ed.
        p. cm. -- (Legal survival guides)
    Includes index.
    ISBN 1-57248-160-9 (pbk.)
    1. Leases--United States--Popular works. 2. Landlord and tenant--United
States--Popular works. I. Title. II. Series.

KF590.Z9 W368 2001
346.7304'346--dc21
                                                            2001040006

Printed and bound in the United States of America.
VHG Paperback — 10 9 8 7 6 5 4 3 2 1

SOUTHWEST WI TECHNICAL COLLEGE
LIBRARY
1800 BRONSON BLVD.
FENNIMORE, WI 53809

U6367

CONTENTS

SOUTHWESTERN TECHNICAL COLLEGE
LIBRARY
1800 BRONSON BLVD,
FENNIMORE, WI 53809

Utilities

Liability

Insurance

Fire or Casualty

Eminent Domain

Assignment and Subletting

Default and Remedies

Notices

Mechanics' or Construction Liens

Fixtures

Guarantee

Miscellaneous Clauses for the Landlord

Miscellaneous Clauses for the Tenant

Using Self-Help Law Books

Before using a self-help law book, you should realize the advantages and disadvantages of doing your own legal work and understand the challenges and diligence that this requires.

THE GROWING TREND

Rest assured that you won't be the first or only person handling your own legal matter. For example, in some states, more than seventy-five percent of divorces and other cases have at least one party representing him or herself. Because of the high cost of legal services, this is a major trend and many courts are struggling to make it easier for people to represent themselves. However, some courts are not happy with people who do not use attorneys and refuse to help them in any way. For some, the attitude is, "Go to the law library and figure it out for yourself."

We at Sphinx write and publish self-help law books to give people an alternative to the often complicated and confusing legal books found in most law libraries. We have made the explanations of the law as simple and easy to understand as possible. Of course, unlike an attorney advising an individual client, we cannot cover every conceivable possibility.

COST/VALUE ANALYSIS

Whenever you shop for a product or service, you are faced with various levels of quality and price. In deciding what product or service to buy, you make a cost/value analysis on the basis of your willingness to pay and the quality you desire.

When buying a car, you decide whether you want transportation, comfort, status, or sex appeal. Accordingly, you decide among such choices as a Neon, a Lincoln, a Rolls Royce, or a Porsche. Before making a decision, you usually weigh the merits of each option against the cost.

When you get a headache, you can take a pain reliever (such as aspirin) or visit a medical specialist for a neurological examination. Given this choice, most people, of course, take a pain reliever, since it costs only pennies; whereas a medical examination costs hundreds of dollars and takes a lot of time. This is usually a logical choice because it is rare to need anything more than a pain reliever for a headache. But in some cases, a headache may indicate a brain tumor and failing to see a specialist right away can result in complications. Should everyone with a headache go to a specialist? Of course not, but people treating their own illnesses must realize that they are betting on the basis of their cost/value analysis of the situation. They are taking the most logical option.

The same cost/value analysis must be made when deciding to do one's own legal work. Many legal situations are very straight forward, requiring a simple form and no complicated analysis. Anyone with a little intelligence and a book of instructions can handle the matter without outside help.

But there is always the chance that complications are involved that only an attorney would notice. To simplify the law into a book like this, several legal cases often must be condensed into a single sentence or paragraph. Otherwise, the book would be several hundred pages long and too complicated for most people. However, this simplification necessarily leaves out many details and nuances that would apply to special or unusual situations. Also, there are many ways to interpret most legal questions. Your case may come before a judge who disagrees with the analysis of our authors.

Therefore, in deciding to use a self-help law book and to do your own legal work, you must realize that you are making a cost/value analysis. You have decided that the money you will save in doing it yourself outweighs the chance that your case will not turn out to your satisfaction. Most people handling their own simple legal matters never have a problem, but occasionally people find that it ended up costing them more to have an attorney straighten out the situation than it would have if they had hired an attorney in the beginning. Keep this in mind if you decide to handle your own case, and be sure to consult an attorney if you feel you might need further guidance.

LOCAL RULES   The next thing to remember is that a book which covers the law for the entire nation, or even for an entire state, cannot possibly include every procedural difference of every county court. Whenever possible, we provide the exact form needed; however, in some areas, each county, or even each judge, may require unique forms and procedures. In our *state* books, our forms usually cover the majority of counties in the state, or provide examples of the type of form that will be required. In our *national* books, our forms are sometimes even more general in nature but are designed to give a good idea of the type of form that will be needed in most locations. Nonetheless, keep in mind that your *state*, county, or judge may have a requirement, or use a form, that is not included in this book.

You should not necessarily expect to be able to get all of the information and resources you need solely from within the pages of this book. This book will serve as your guide, giving you specific information whenever possible and helping you to find out what else you will need to know. This is just like if you decided to build your own backyard deck. You might purchase a book on how to build decks. However, such a book would not include the building codes and permit requirements of every city, town, county, and township in the nation; nor would it include the lumber, nails, saws, hammers, and other materials and tools you would need to actually build the deck. You would use the book as your guide, and then do some work and research involving such matters as whether you need a permit of some kind, what type and grade of wood are available in your area, whether to use hand tools or power tools, and how to use those tools.

Before using the forms in a book like this, you should check with your court clerk to see if there are any local rules of which you should be aware, or local forms you will need to use. Often, such forms will require the same information as the forms in the book but are merely laid out differently, use slightly different language, or use different color paper so the clerks can easily find them. They will sometimes require additional information.

CHANGES IN
THE LAW

Besides being subject to state and local rules and practices, the law is subject to change at any time. The courts and the legislatures of all fifty states are constantly revising the laws. It is possible that while you are reading this book, some aspect of the law is being changed or that a court is interpreting a law in a different way. You should always check the most recent statutes, rules and regulations to see what, if any changes have been made.

In most cases, the change will be of minimal significance. A form will be redesigned, additional information will be required, or a waiting period will be extended. As a result, you might need to revise a form, file an extra form, or wait out a longer time period; these types of changes will not usually affect the outcome of your case. On the other hand, sometimes a major part of the law is changed, the entire law in a particular area is rewritten, or a case that was the basis of a central legal point is overruled. In such instances, your entire ability to pursue your case may be impaired.

Again, you should weigh the value of your case against the cost of an attorney and make a decision as to what you believe is in your best interest.

INTRODUCTION

Standard printed lease forms do not always serve the needs of the parties. Some are so weak they lead to problems. Some are so tough they would be thrown out of court. A good lease should be tailored to the needs of both of the parties.

This book provides an explanation of various versions of each type of clause used in real estate leases. You can use this book to evaluate the clauses in your lease, or to put together a lease of your own. Also included are some form leases which may be useful in many situations.

Chapters 1 and 2 of this book explain the positions of the parties and the laws that control their rights when signing real estate leases. Chapters 3 through 6 explain the laws that apply when leasing real property. Chapters 7 through 9 contain various types of clauses and explanations of what they mean for residential and commercial situations. Chapter 10 includes specific information regarding storage space leases. The appendix includes several forms such as a house lease, an apartment lease, two different commercial leases, and a storage space lease.

NOTE: *Since the words* lessor *and* lessee *are easily confused, we have used* Landlord *and* Tenant *throughout the book.*

Because there are so many different government agencies issuing rules and regulations of all kinds, it is impossible for a book of this type to cover every requirement in every locality. It is possible that your city, county, or state government has passed some law requiring you to, or prohibiting you from, using certain clauses. To find out, you should check with a local attorney, real estate management company, or Board of Realtors®. You might be able to get a list of laws from a local government official, but do not rely on it being complete. To dig a little deeper yourself, you can check your state statutes and local ordinances at a public library or law library.

Finally, before signing a lease, or any legal document, be sure you understand the legal ramifications of each clause. If you are not certain about something, then you should have it reviewed by an attorney.

THE LANDLORD'S POSITION 1

In most areas of the country the landlord has nearly complete control of the terms of the lease when he rents real property, such as a house, apartment, or store. This has been the system for hundreds of years and this custom is very difficult to change. From the landlord's view this is the way it should be. The landlord has thousands of dollars invested in the property and he or she does not want to turn it over to a complete stranger without strong legal protection.

MOM-AND-POP LANDLORDS

Some people have a negative attitude toward landlords. However, most landlords today are just middle class people who invested some of their savings in a rental house because they thought it would offer a better return than a bank account. Many landlords bought their properties with little money down and have substantial mortgages on them. When tenants miss a month's rent, or landlords have to do a major repair, the money comes out of the landlords' paychecks. So for them, it makes sense to give the landlord control over the terms of the lease.

Rent Control

Unfortunately, in some areas of the country the local governments have taken rights away from landlords and imposed rent controls and other similar laws. So far they have been upheld by the courts, including even the U. S. Supreme Court, but there is hope among some that the current court will soon strike them down as a violation of property rights. Our constitution requires that whenever property is taken by the government the owner must be compensated. There is a good argument that rent control laws take away property by making it less valuable and that landlords should be compensated by the government for this.

If you own property in an area subject to rent control, then you may not be able to use all of the clauses or suggestions in this book. You should check with the local rent control board for their latest rules and regulations. You should also keep up on developments in the law and consider joining with other landlords to challenge the laws. If you are ever unsure about a law, contact an attorney.

Bad Faith and Unconscionable Leases

In most areas of the country the landlord is free to set most of the lease terms unless they are outrageous or unconscionable. Years ago contracts were enforced on their terms, no matter how unfair they were. Today courts will refuse to enforce agreements that are considered "shocking to the conscience," or made in *bad faith*. In some states there are laws specifically prohibiting leases that are *unconscionable*. What exactly is unconscionable? It all depends upon the judge, jury, and facts of your case. There is no hard and fast rule you can follow.

From the landlord's point of view the lease should be as strong as possible without being so harsh that it is in danger of being held invalid by a court. Just what is too strong is a matter of state law. States differ greatly in what they allow, and what is legal in one state may be unconscionable in another.

If you plan to use a very strong lease, it might be in danger of being held invalid by a court. You should check your state laws before using it. The state laws on the subject usually consist of the state landlord/tenant statutes along with court cases interpreting the statutes and covering areas of law not included in the statutes.

To check the laws in your state you should get a copy of your state statutes and a summary of the most recent cases. Statutes should be available from your secretary of state or can be copied in a public library or law library. (The major landlord/tenant statute sections for each state are listed in Chapter 5 on page ___.) To research the cases you can hire a lawyer or paralegal, or if you have the time, you might want to spend an afternoon in a law library reading them yourself. In some states, such as California and Florida, there are books available explaining landlord/tenant law. In most states there are *digests*, which are collections of summaries of cases sorted by subject.

Some landlords use leases that are not very strong without ever having any trouble. But landlords who have had a bad experience with tenants prefer strongly worded leases so that they can get rid of the tenants quickly. The rationale is that few tenants know their rights or can afford an attorney to protect those rights. The landlords gamble that their iron-clad lease will work in most instances and will not ever get to court. If it ever does get to court, they figure they will settle out of court, giving the tenant some concession.

Another tactic used by some landlords is to use "self-help" methods such as taking the doors off the property or having the electricity turned off. The trouble with these strategies is that in most areas there are laws protecting tenants from landlords and some of these give the tenant substantial *damages* (money) and attorney's fees. In some states tenants can get thousands of dollars in *punitive* damages from a landlord who has the utilities shut off (punitive damages are sums of money that must be paid as punishment). In many areas tenants are allowed free legal aid (paid for in part by landlords' taxes and the interest on funds held in attorneys' trust accounts). These legal aid lawyers sometimes delay the case and get the landlord to pay higher attorney's fees.

SEVERABILITY

One important clause to have in a lease is a *severability clause*. This is a clause that states that if one of the clauses in the lease is held to be illegal or unenforceable, then that will not affect the validity of the rest of the lease. Without a severability clause, it is possible to have an entire lease thrown out for one bad clause.

THE BEST STRATEGY

The best strategy for a landlord to use is to have a lease that is strong but fair, to screen tenants carefully, and to get as large a security deposit as possible.

SCREENING

Tenant Application. You should use a tenant application that gives you enough information to decide if the tenant is a good risk and to find him or her if he or she leaves without fulfilling the terms of the lease. For screening the tenant, you should get rental addresses and landlord's names prior to the current address. To be able to track the tenant down later, you should get a driver's license, social security, and bank account numbers.

NOTE: *You should not ask any questions about race, nationality, age, disabilities, or anything else that might be illegally discriminatory.*

A TENANT APPLICATION form is included in this book, which should be useful in most areas. (see form 1, p.___.) However, you should check local law to see if any of the information is not allowed.

Credit Report. In some areas credit bureaus offer special rates on tenant credit reports. These can be as low as $10 or even $5. When weighed against the cost of an eviction or damage to the property the cost is meaningless, but it is amazing how many landlords will not part with $10 to protect their property. Some landlords avoid the cost altogether by charging a non-refundable application fee. To find a source of reports on tenants you should check your yellow pages under "credit reports" or "credit bureaus." Or, call a local landlords' association or the manager of a large apartment complex.

Screening Companies. There are also a number of companies that specialize in tenant screening. Some even guarantee that the tenant will not default or they pay for the eviction. Ask at your landlords' association if these services are available in your area.

SECURITY
DEPOSIT

Most landlords know the difficulty of getting a large security deposit out of a tenant. With lower priced rentals you may find most tenants do not have money for a deposit and want to pay $10 or $25 per week toward the deposit. In such cases you must use your own judgment. You may be lucky and have it work out fine. Then again the tenant may never pay, damage the apartment, and use stalling tactics to keep him in the place for months. Of course, there are many state laws controlling security deposits, so you should be sure to look up and follow the rules.

LEASE
COMPONENTS

Other important things a landlord should have in a lease are as follows:

- prohibition on assignment or subleasing;

- limit on the number of occupants;

- clear definition of and remedy for default; and

- right to access to the premises.

Some states have laws spelling out the parties' rights in these areas, but it is also good to include them in the lease so that the law is clear to the tenant. There are many other things that should be included in a lease to protect the landlord from an unfavorable situation. These are explained in Chapters 6, 7, and 8. Be sure to review all the clauses.

PARTIES TO THE LEASE

Before drafting a lease, you should consider who will legally be the other party. If a couple is renting the unit, then you should get the signatures of both on the lease. This way you have the assets of both guaranteeing payment even if they break up and one leaves.

If you rent to a corporation, then you should get the personal guaranties of the officers or shareholders. Often a corporation will be a shell with few assets and will allow the principals to walk away from the lease without liability. If the market is *soft* (many vacant units), then you might consider accepting a corporation without personal guaranties if the alternative is to let the unit sit vacant. A large security deposit would make this situation even more acceptable.

TENANTS' LEASES

Most tenants will expect to sign a landlord's lease and most will not even question the terms. Occasionally a tenant might want to make a change in a lease or to offer his or her own lease. Whether a landlord should agree to either of these would depend upon how tight the rental market is and how serious the changes are.

It is usually a bad idea to sign a tenant's own lease. If a tenant took the trouble to prepare his or her own lease there is a good chance that it contains all kinds of protections for the tenant, possibly even some unconscionable clauses. Innocent-looking clauses may end up costing the landlord a bundle. Let the tenant suggest changes to your lease, but do not sign a tenant's lease.

THE TENANT'S POSITION 2

In most cases tenants do not have a lot of control over the terms of a lease of real property. Historically leases have been "take-it-or-leave-it" legal documents. However, where the rental market is soft many landlords will gladly give in on a few points to get a good tenant. This is especially true in commercial rentals. Many areas of the country are overbuilt in commercial rentals, and landlords are giving considerable concessions to get new tenants.

CONCESSIONS

Even in residential rentals it is often possible to get concessions. Most landlords use form leases and many do not understand all of the clauses themselves. Landlords lose money every day a rental unit sits vacant and if you look like a good tenant and offer a reasonable compromise in a lease, it might be accepted. This is especially true if the market is soft or the unit has been vacant for a long time. "It can't hurt to ask" is a theory you should use when negotiating a lease. Many tenants have been very pleasantly surprised when they asked for concessions from a landlord.

Tenants rarely offer their own leases and landlords would probably not accept them in most cases, but again, it cannot hurt to ask. A situation where it would be most likely that you would be able to use your own lease form would be where the owner of a property was not experienced in leasing it.

Example: If you approached a landowner about renting an unused part of his field, or if a widow owned a vacant store where her spouse had a business, then you could make an offer to rent it and even provide your own lease form.

UNCONSCIONABLE OR UNENFORCEABLE LEASES

In the previous chapter landlords are warned about unconscionable leases. If a lease is so unfair that it is shocking to an ordinary person it can be held illegal or unenforceable in many areas. This would usually be true even if a tenant supplied the lease form.

However, there are not many situations in which a tenant could get so good a deal that it would be unconscionable. The biggest danger is that the lease could be held *unenforceable*. There is a legal principle (discussed in more detail in Chapter 4) that holds that a contract must be enforceable by both sides. If you give yourself a loophole to get out of the lease whenever you want, then the landlord will probably also be able to cancel the lease at any time.

The following are some of the most important things for a tenant to look for in a lease:

- grace period for late payments/no automatic termination;

- no automatic forfeiture of any money; and

- cancellation of the lease if the premises are unusable.

There are many other clauses that are important to have or to avoid. You should be sure to read the explanation of individual clauses in Chapters 7, 8 and 9. Be sure to read every clause in a lease you are considering signing and do not sign the lease unless you understand them.

One of the most common questions asked of lawyers by tenants is whether leases are *enforceable*. In most cases the answer is yes. That is the purpose of a lease; to obligate both parties for a set term. If you sign a lease and leave before the end of the term it may be possible for the landlord to let the unit sit vacant and sue you for the rent, even if the lease is five years long!

LAWSUIT AND JUDGMENTS

If you have no money or property, then a landlord may not bother suing you, especially if a new tenant is found quickly. But in most states a judgment is good for many years. If a landlord sues you for breaking a lease, then you may have a judgment filed against you for thousands of dollars including back rent (possibly double rent), damages to the property, court costs, and attorney's fees. This may ruin your credit, or it may even turn into a lien on property you inherit ten or twenty years in the future.

If you are sued by a landlord, then you should not ignore the suit. If you are not properly served with notice of the suit, then the landlord may be unable to get a judgment against you, but once you have been properly served the landlord can be granted everything he asks for unless you object. If the landlord asks for more rent than is owed, more damages than you caused, or late fees that are not owed, then the judge will grant them unless you present your side of the case.

PERSONAL LIABILITY

CORPORATIONS
In a commercial rental, one way to avoid the risk of personal liability is to have a corporation sign the lease. Unfortunately, most landlords will also want a personal guaranty from the owners of the corporation. However, with an unsophisticated or desperate landlord, you may get by without the guaranty. In a soft market you have a good argument that the landlord should be happy with the rent as long as the business

is in operation, and that he will not need your personal funds once the unit becomes vacant.

SPOUSES In both commercial and residential rentals it is often best from the tenant's point of view to have only one spouse sign the lease. This is especially true if one spouse has substantial assets. If both sign a lease, then the landlord could go after property owned by either or both of them. With only one signature, the property of the other would be safe and in some states property owned jointly would be safe.

The Art of Negotiating 3

In some societies negotiation is a way of life and an exciting challenge. People are offended if you accept their first offer. They want you to complain and to counteroffer. They love to haggle and to feel they have gotten the best deal they could get out of you.

This is not true in America. Most Americans hate haggling. Haggling means uncertainty and the possibility of rejection. We never know how high or how low to go and we always worry if we could have gotten a better deal. We would much rather know the bottom line so we can take it or leave it. (Recently a car dealer greatly expanded his business by marking its lowest prices on the cars and *not* negotiating.)

Fortunately for Americans, not much negotiating is done in real estate rentals. Landlords offer their lease and tenants take it or leave it. This is especially true in residential tenancies. Some tenants do not even read the lease. The only factor of concern is the rental rate and they do not even realize that that may be negotiable.

But negotiation of a real estate lease can mean a profit or savings of thousands of dollars. The rule you should use in entering into a lease is "It can't hurt to ask." By using this motto you can reap considerable benefits. Sometimes this can be in monthly rent but it can also be made in other terms of the lease.

If you want to get serious about negotiating, there are several good books on the market explaining all the techniques and nuances of negotiation. If a lot of money is involved you might want to get one of these or to hire the services of an attorney or broker to negotiate for you. If not, you can just tailor the ideas and techniques in this chapter to your considerable advantage.

BEST/WORST

First, you should figure out what is the best deal you can hope for (best supportable position) and what is the least that you would accept (worst acceptable position). With these figures you have a range within which to aim and you will know immediately if the deal is worthwhile. Without this you will negotiate aimlessly and may end up with a bad deal.

You should make a list of all the factors which support your best position and use them to argue your case. Use your imagination and come up with as many reasons as possible. When people aim high they often end up high. Asking a lot for something gives the other side the perception, correct or not, that it is worth a lot.

NOTE: *The position must be supportable. Do not make a ridiculous offer that no one in their right mind would accept. Otherwise you might not be taken seriously, or they might not even bother negotiating with you.*

If you ask too high and the other side accepts, they may be unable to fulfill the deal. If you, as the landlord, demand too much rent for a store the tenant may not be able to afford to advertise and may go out of business. Or, if as a tenant you extract too many concessions from a desperate landlord, the property may go into foreclosure and the bank may cancel your lease.

Keep in mind that your worst acceptable position may change. If an offer is made that meets some of your other needs, one part of your position may be worth changing.

Example: If you are looking for a place to open a restaurant and the most you want to pay is $1000 a month, you may reconsider a place offered for $1100 if the landlord offers to lock in the rent for five years, provide additional storage space, or give you the first two months rent-free.

Need versus Position

One of the biggest mistakes in negotiation is to concentrate on your position and ignore your need. Once people have stated a position it becomes a matter of pride to maintain that position. In some societies saving face may be important. You must decide if you are more interested in saving face or in making a good deal. You should analyze the situation, determine your need, and concentrate on that need.

Example: Your position may be that you want $1000 a month rent and you must refuse a tenant who offers $950. But your actual need may be to cover your expenses and not have negative cash flow. Therefore if you can get the tenant to take care of the lawn (saving you $50 a month) you can accept the $950 rent offer. If you concentrate only on your position—$1000 a month minimum—you might lose a good deal.

Sometimes your goals may not be clear even to yourself. If you are interested in renting a certain apartment but the price is too high, perhaps getting the price down is not your only option. The landlord may have a lower priced unit in a building even closer to your job. Examine your position and decide exactly what is most important to you.

Understanding the Other Side

You can negotiate much better if you understand the other side's position and the motivation behind it. In other words, as explained in the last paragraph, what is their need? If you are the tenant wanting to pay no more than $950 in rent and the landlord wants $1000, what is his need?

Figure out the other side's bottom line need and why that is it. Understand their interests and try to formulate your offer to fill their interests as well as yours.

Similarly you should not let the other side know your need. Otherwise they will figure out your worst possible position and try to stick you with it. You should concentrate on your best possible position and divert the other side away from factors that reveal your worst possible position.

Remember that the other side may feel it is important to protect his or her position. Make your offer in such a way as to make them happy to accept it. One way to do this is to make it look like you are making a big change in your position to accommodate them.

EMOTIONAL INVOLVEMENT WITH THE DEAL

The best negotiators are those who do not need the deal, and the worst ones are those who must have it. If you are ready to walk away from the deal if you do not get what you want, and the other side feels it, you will do much better. On the other hand if you have already decided that you must have this deal, then you are easy pickings.

If you are also considering other properties or other tenants, you will not be pressed to take this one. Even if you do not have others you can at least act like you do.

TAKING THINGS PERSONALLY

Another mistake in negotiating is to get personally involved with your opponent. After meeting with them a few times you may have developed a rapport, or found out that you have things in common, and you may feel awkward in not accepting whatever they offer. It is not easy to turn some-one down, especially someone who has just become your friend. So you must first decide if you want to make a profit or a new friend.

Some people are soft negotiators and others hard. Some give in easily just to avoid disagreement and others hold out until they get everything they want. If you are the former, you will easily be taken advantage of by the latter.

AGENTS   One way to avoid such a situation is to negotiate through an agent. It is easy for an agent to become best friends with the tenant and support the tenant's position, but to explain that he has no control over the landlord's decision. Some landlords even tell the tenant that they are only the managers of the property in order to maintain a better relationship. One advantage of using a *land trust* (a passive trust used in some states to hold title to real estate) is that the landlord can be friendly with the tenant and explain that the trust has certain rules that must be followed. This is beyond the scope of this book.

"GOOD GUY/BAD GUY" APPROACH

Another variation is to use the "good guy/bad guy" approach.

Example: A property owned by a couple is advertised to rent at $500, though they would accept $475. A prospective tenant approaches and says he can only afford $450. If the husband gets upset, says it is worth $550 and storms out of the room, the wife can apologize for him and say he is never reasonable but she might be able to convince him to accept $475.

Do not lock into a position, otherwise each change will be difficult. Keep in mind the worst acceptable result that you have already established and do not worry about the intermediate steps. Be open to all possible options and any new suggestions the other side may have. There may be an alternative that you have not even considered.

Keep in mind that the other side may be taking his or her side personally. Do not criticize the other side personally or say anything that makes the other side more attached to their position.

STARTING POSITION

Start at your best supportable position. This may sound obvious, but some people give away their worst acceptable position right away. Keep in mind that "it can't hurt to ask" and try your best supportable position. Many people have started with ridiculously high figures and have been surprised to have them accepted.

You only get one chance to state your opening position and you usually cannot go higher. Suppose you have a strip center with one store soon to be vacant. If you advertise it at $1000 a month and fifty people immediately offer to rent it you will know you started too low, but it will be hard to ask for more once you advertise it at $1000.

TURNING THE TABLES

Whether you are the landlord or tenant, when you enter negotiations for a rental the other side will probably expect to do the screening. The landlord will be wanting to screen for a good tenant and the tenant will want to be sure the unit meets his or her needs.

If you begin the negotiation by listing your needs and asking if the other side can meet them, then you have turned the tables. The other side will then be put in the position of wondering if they can match your needs. Meeting your needs will then be the primary goal and their needs may be forgotten.

Example: If you are a landlord and greet a prospective tenant with questions such as, "How long have you been at your job?" or "How long have you been living in your present apartment?" then the tenant's first question is whether he qualifies to rent the place. Maybe its not exactly what he wanted but the thought of not being able to have it makes it seem more valuable.

YOUR LAST SHOT

Once you think you may be able to make a deal, why not ask for one last concession? If you like the apartment, the rent is acceptable, and the landlord will repaint two of the rooms, try something like, "Those kitchen curtains are really ugly. Put up new curtains and I will take it." (It can't hurt to ask.)

FEDERAL LAWS 4

Although most of the laws regulating the leasing of real property are state statutes and cases, there are also federal laws that govern many types of rentals. These are mostly discrimination laws. The penalties for violation of these laws are quite severe so you should be careful to avoid even the appearance of a violation. Even if you win a case filed against you, it could cost you thousands of dollars in attorney's fees.

One area of federal law that does not concern discrimination is environmental law. Owners of property are being fined hundreds of thousands or even millions of dollars for the cleanup of toxic substances. Landlords should be careful that in renting their property they do not allow a tenant to cause any environmental damage to the property.

LEAD-BASED PAINT NOTICE LAW

In 1996, the Environmental Protection Agency and the Department of Housing and Urban Development issued regulations requiring notices to be given to tenants of rental housing built before 1978. These notices state that there may be lead-based paint present and that it could pose a health hazard to children. This applies to all housing except housing for the elderly or zero-bedroom units (efficiencies, studio apartments, etc.) It also requires that a pamphlet titled *Protect Your Family from Lead in Your Home,* be given to prospective tenants. The recommended LEAD-BASED PAINT DISCLOSURE form is included in this book. (see form 13, p. 193.) The pamphlet is also included. (see page 151.)

The rule is contained in the Federal Register (FR), Volume 61, Number 45, (March 6, 1996), pages 9064 through 9088. More information can be obtained from the National Lead Information Clearinghouse at 800-424-5323. The information can also be obtained on the Internet at:

http://www.hud.gov/lea/leadhelp.html

DISCRIMINATION

CIVIL RIGHTS ACT OF 1968

The Civil Rights Act of 1968 makes it illegal to discriminate on the basis of race, sex, religion, or nationality in the rental of real property. (United States Code (U.S.C.), Title 42, Section (Sec.) 3601-17.) Even policies that do not clearly discriminate, but have the effect of discriminating, are illegal under this law.

Penalty. A victim of discrimination under this section can file a civil suit, a HUD complaint, or request the U.S. Attorney General to prosecute. Damages can include actual losses and punitive damages of up to $1000.

Limitation. The complaint must be brought within 180 days.

Exemptions. This law does not apply to owners of three or fewer single family homes if there is no more than one sale in twenty-four months, if the owner does not own any interest in more than three at one time, and if no real estate agent or discriminatory advertisement is used. It also does not apply to property that the owner lives in if it has four or less units.

Coercion or Intimidation. Where coercion or intimidation is used to bring about discrimination there is no limit to when the action can be brought or the amount of damages.

● A violation of the law occurred when a real estate agent was fired for renting to a black tenant. *Wilkey v. Pyramid Construction Co.,* 619 F.S. 1453 (D. Conn. 1983).

CIVIL RIGHTS
ACT SECTION
1982

The Civil Rights Act Section 1982 is a law similar to the above statute. (U.S.C., Title 42, Sec. 1982.) This law applies only where it can be proved that the person had an intent to discriminate, whereas the above applies to any policy that has a discriminatory effect.

Penalty. Damages can include actual damages plus unlimited *punitive* damages.

Limitation. There are none.

Exemptions. There are none.

CIVIL RIGHTS
AND CHILDREN

In 1988, the Civil Rights Act was amended to ban discrimination against the handicapped and families with children. (U.S.C., Title 42, Sec. 3601.) While refusing to rent to families with children may protect the value and condition of your property, such discrimination can now result in very high fines. Congress and President Reagan decided that families with children have more rights than owners of property.

Penalty. Penalties include $10,000 for the first offense, $25,000 for the second violation within five years, and up to $50,000 for three or more violations within seven years. Unlimited punitive damages can be awarded in private actions.

Limitation. A complaint can be brought within two years for private actions.

Exemptions. This law does not apply to single family homes if the owner owns three or fewer, if there is no more than one sale within twenty-four months, and no real estate agent or discriminatory advertisement is used. A condominium unit is not defined as a single-family home so it is not exempt. It also does not apply to property in which the owner lives if it has four or less units. Additionally there are exemptions for dwellings in state and federal programs for the elderly, for complexes that are solely

SOUTHWEST WI TECHNICAL COLLEGE
LIBRARY
1800 BRONSON BLVD. 46367
FENNIMORE, WI 53809

used by persons sixty-two or older, for complexes used solely by persons fifty-five or over if there are substantial facilities designed for the elderly, for religious housing, and for private clubs.

CIVIL RIGHTS
AND DISABILITY

In 1992, the Americans with Disabilities Act took effect. It puts the extra costs and burdens of accommodating the needs of the disabled on the businesses and landlords with whom they come in contact. Formerly, legislation that was aimed at helping various groups in society was paid for with tax dollars. Politicians have found a way to give out benefits without calling the cost a tax.

This law requires that "reasonable accommodations" be made to provide access to commercial premises for the disabled and it forbids discrimination against them. This means that the disabled must be able to get to, enter, and use the facilities in commercial premises. It requires that if access is "readily achievable" without *undue burden* or *undue hardship* (not so costly that it puts someone out of business) then changes must be made to the property to make it accessible.

If any commercial premises are remodeled, then the remodeling must include modifications that make the premises accessible. All new construction must also meet the requirements of the law.

The law does not clearly define what these terms mean and does not even explain exactly who will qualify as handicapped. Some say that up to 40% of America's labor force may qualify as handicapped in some way. The law includes people with emotional illnesses, AIDS, dyslexia, past alcohol or drug addictions, as well as hearing, sight, and mobility impairments.

What is reasonable will usually depend upon the size of the business. Small businesses will not have to make major alterations to their premises if the expense would be an undue hardship. Even large businesses will not have to make all shelving low enough for people in wheelchairs to reach as long as there is an employee to help the person. In addition there are tax credits for businesses of less than thirty employees and less than $1 million in sales. For more information on these credits, obtain IRS forms 8826 and 3800 and their instructions by calling 800-829-3676 or from the Internet at:

http://www.irs.gov

Some of the changes that must be made to property to make it more accessible to the disabled are:

- installing ramps;
- widening doorways;
- making curb cuts in sidewalks;
- repositioning shelves;
- repositioning telephones;
- removing high pile, low density carpeting; and
- installing a full-length bathroom mirror.

Both the landlord and the tenant can be liable if the changes are not made to the premises. Most likely the landlord would be liable for common areas and the tenant for the area under his control. However, since previous leases did not address this new statute, either party could conceivably be held liable.

Penalty. Injunctions and fines of $50,000 for the first offense or $100,000 for subsequent offenses can be awarded.

Exemptions. Private clubs and religious organizations are exempt from this law.

STATE AND LOCAL LAWS 5

More and more laws are being passed in this country which control all types of behavior and many of these affect the rental of real estate. States, counties, towns, and villages are making laws to cover every type of problem that comes up between people. Often these laws cause more problems then they prevent.

This chapter explains the most common laws that apply when leasing property. Since laws and local rules change frequently and are issued by various state and local government agencies it would be impossible to list every rule in the U.S. in this type of book. To be sure you comply with the rules you should check with a local attorney, real estate manager, or government office that provides information to landlords and tenants.

LANDLORD/TENANT STATUTES

Every state has statutes that cover landlord/tenant relations. Most of these cover problems such as late rent and evictions, but some have rules that apply to the lease. If you are a landlord you should have a copy of your state's landlord/tenant law so that you are sure not to break any of the rules. Even innocent violations can cost a landlord thousands of dollars.

The following are citations to major landlord/tenant laws for each state.

NOTE: *Some states have both statutes and annotated statutes. Annotated statutes have a summary of the relevant court cases along with each statute. If you want to look up the interpretation of a statute use the annotated version. Since the annotated statutes can run hundreds of pages, for home use you will probably want to photocopy just the statutes.*

Alabama	Code of Alabama, beginning with Section 35-9-1
Alaska	Alaska Statutes, Sections 34.03.010 to 34.03.380
Arizona	Arizona Revised Statutes, Sections 12-1171 to 12-1183; Sections 33-1301 to 33-1381
Arkansas	Arkansas Code Annotated, Sections 18-16-101 to 12-306
California	California Civil Code, Sections 1925-1954, 1961-1962.7, 1995.010-1997.270
Colorado	Colorado Revised Statutes, Sections 38-12-101 to 38-12-104, -38-12-301 to 18-12-302
Connecticut	General Statutes of Connecticut, Sections 47a-1 to -50a
Delaware	Delaware Code, Title 25, Sections 5101-7013
D. C.	District of Columbia Code, Sections 45-1401 to 45-1597, 45-2501 to 45-2593
Florida	Florida Statutes, Chapter 83
Georgia	Code of Georgia, beginning with Section 44-7-1
Hawaii	Hawaii Revised Statutes, beginning with Section 521-1
Idaho	Idaho Code, Sections 6-301 to 6-324; Sections 55-201 to 55-313
Illinois	Illinois Compiled Statutes, Chapter 765, Paragraph 705/0.01-740/5
Indiana	Indiana Code Annotated, Sections 32-7-1-1 to 37-7-19
Iowa	Iowa Code Annotated, Sections 562A.1-.36

Kansas	Kansas Statutes Annotated, Sections 58-2501 to 58-2573
Kentucky	Kentucky Revised Statutes, Sections 383.010-.715
Louisiana	Louisiana Revised Statutes, Sections 9:3201-9:3259
	Louisiana Civil Code, Article 2669-2742
Maine	Maine Revised Statutes, Title 14, Sections 6001-6045
Maryland	Annotated Code of Maryland, Real Property, Sections 8-101 to 8-604
Massachusetts	Massachusetts General Laws Annotated, Chapter 186, Sections 1-21
Michigan	Michigan Compiled Laws Annotated, Section 554.601-.640
Minnesota	Minnesota Statutes Annotated, Sections 504B.01 to 504B.471
Mississippi	Mississippi Code, beginning with Section 89-8-1
Missouri	Missouri Annotated Statutes, Sections 441.010-.650; Sections 535.150-.300
Montana	Montana Code Annotated, Sections 70-24-101 to 70-25-206
Nebraska	Nebraska Revised Statutes, Sections 76-1401 to 76-1449
Nevada	Nevada Revised Statutes Annotated, Sections 18A.010-.520
New Hampshire	New Hampshire Revised Statutes Annotated, Sections 540:1 to 540:29; 540-A:1-540-A:8
New Jersey	New Jersey Statutes Annotated, beginning with Section 46:8-1
New Mexico	New Mexico Statutes Annotated, beginning with Section 47-8-1

New York	New York Real Property Law, Sections 220-338;
	Real Property Actions and Proceedings Law, Section 701-853
	Multiple Dwelling Law
	Multiple Residence Law
	General Obligation Law, Sections 7-103-108
North Carolina	North Carolina General Statutes, Sections 42-1 to 42-14.2; 42-25-6 to 42-76
North Dakota	North Dakota Century Code, Sections 47-16-01 to 47-16-41
Ohio	Ohio Revised Code, Sections 5321.01-.19
Oklahoma	Oklahoma Statutes, Title 41, Sections 1-136
Oregon	Oregon Revised Statutes, Sections 90.100-.450
Pennsylvania	Pennsylvania Statutes, Title 68, Sections 250.101-.510-B
Rhode Island	General Laws of Rhode Island, Sections 34-18-1 to 34-18-57
South Carolina	Code of Laws of South Carolina, Sections 27-40-10 to 27-40-910
South Dakota	South Dakota Codified Laws, beginning with Section 43-32-1
Tennessee	Tennessee Code Annotated, Sections 66-28-101 to 66-28-520
Texas	Texas Property Code, Sections 91.001-92.354
Utah	Utah Code Annotated, Sections 57-17-1 to 57-17-5, 57-17-22-1 to 57-17-6
Vermont	Vermont Statutes Annotated, Title 9, Sections 4451-4468
Virginia	Code of Virginia, Sections 55-218.1 to 55-248.40

Washington	Washington Revised Code Annotated, Sections 59.04.010-.900, 59.18.010-.910
West Virginia	West Virginia Code, Sections 37-6-1 to 37-6-30
Wisconsin	Wisconsin Statutes Annotated, Sections 704.01-704.45
Wyoming	Wyoming Statutes, Sections 1-2-12-1 to 1-21-1211; 34-2-128 to 34-2-129

SECURITY DEPOSIT LAWS

Many states have laws covering security deposits. A few cities (those with rent control) also have such laws. The laws in many states limit how much deposit you can require. Some require separate accounts and a few require the payment of interest to tenants. (While landlords can sometimes only receive 2% or 3% interest from their banks today, in some cities landlords are required by law to pay tenants 5% or more on their deposit!)

The following states have laws limiting the amount of deposit that can be required:

Alaska	Kansas	New Hampshire
Arizona	Louisiana	New Jersey
Arkansas	Maine	New Mexico
California	Maryland	North Carolina
Connecticut	Massachusetts	North Dakota
Delaware	Michigan	Pennsylvania
D. C.	Missouri	Rhode Island
Hawaii	Nebraska	South Dakota
Iowa	Nevada	Virginia

Some states have exemptions for small landlords. Some states have certain requirements that must be followed if a landlord wants to keep the security deposit. If you do not follow the law to the letter, then the tenant gets his deposit back plus attorney's fees, even if he destroyed your property.

DISCRIMINATION

In addition to the federal discrimination laws, many states and municipalities have their own laws. The rationale is that while federal remedies may be difficult to enforce, a local law can provide more protection. Some of these laws are even stricter than the federal laws and include more categories, such as "sexual orientation." In some areas, such as Dade County, Florida, the age discrimination law is so strict that it has made it impossible to build housing for the elderly.

ACCESS

Due to some inconsiderate landlords walking unannounced into their tenant's bedrooms, there are laws in some areas regulating when a landlord may enter a unit. Many of these require "reasonable notice." If there is no law giving the landlord a right to access and a lease does not grant access to the landlord, then he has no right to enter the premises until the end of the lease. Whether or not there is a law, it is important to spell out the landlord's rights in the lease. This way there can be no disagreements or hard feelings.

RENT CONTROL

In some communities in four states and in the District of Columbia, there are laws regulating the amount of rent that a landlord may charge. Those states are California, Maryland, New Jersey, and New York. If you own rental property in an area covered by rent control, then you should obtain the applicable rules from the rent control board or an apartment owners' association.

LIABILITY

Some states have laws forbidding landlords from protecting themselves from liability for their own acts with clauses in the lease. In some cases this may mean that such a clause in a lease will merely be ignored. Where this is the case, using such a clause may still provide some protection from tenants who read the clause and do not bother to make a claim. However, in some cases such a clause may give a judge an excuse to void the entire lease or grant other rights to a tenant.

MAINTENANCE

Many areas have laws that require landlords to take care of certain maintenance on the premises. In some cases the landlord may overrule the law by stating otherwise in the lease, but in other cases the law overrules the lease. In some areas the landlord may have the tenant handle the maintenance in a single family home, or two- or three-unit buildings, but not in a larger apartment building.

REPAIR AND DEDUCT

In some states, when a landlord fails to do maintenance on the premises the tenant is allowed to have it done by a third party and can deduct the cost from the rent. In some cases the lease may overrule the law by stating that the tenant agrees to do all maintenance at his or her expense.

DISCLOSURE

Several states have laws requiring certain disclosures to tenants, such as if a tenant's electric bill covers lights in the hallway as well as his apartment. Georgia and Oklahoma require disclosure of whether the unit was subject to flooding during the last five years. Florida requires the disclosure of the person authorized to receive notices from the tenants for the landlord, and in buildings exceeding three stories, the availability of fire protection. California requires disclosure that a person can obtain information from the state on sex offenders living in the area. Hawaii requires disclosure of the landlord's excise tax number.

WATER BEDS

In many areas there are laws that a landlord cannot forbid water beds in their units. Fortunately, the landlord can usually require the tenant to buy insurance in case the water bed causes damage to the property.

LANGUAGE

Some states have laws that require that if a lease is negotiated in a language other than English it must be written in that language.

UTILITIES

In some states if a tenant's utility bill covers more than just his or her unit, then the lease is required to explain exactly what areas are paid for by the tenant.

RADON

In some states, laws require that every lease contain a mention of possible hazard from radon gas. While this may seem like something the landlord would not want to do, it is actually a protection for the landlord against litigation. Like the warnings on cigarette packages, it may protect the landlord if the tenant later wants to sue for damages.

ASBESTOS

In some states the landlord is required to disclose to the tenant the presence of asbestos in the premises. Giving such notice can protect the landlord from liability, but it may scare away a prospective tenant.

TERMINATION

State law often controls when and how a tenancy may be terminated. When there is a lease for a fixed term the landlord usually must give a certain notice before terminating the lease for default. Even where the tenancy is month-to-month the law may spell out how many days notice must be given before it may be terminated.

Example: In some states, fifteen days notice must be given to terminate a month-to-month tenancy. But often a tenancy cannot be terminated in the middle of a monthly term. Thus, if a landlord gave a notice of termination on January 20th, the tenant could stay until February 28th. That is because January 20th did not give the tenant the required fifteen days before the end of the term.

FORMS

In some areas lease forms or other forms or notices are required or recommended by law. These may include lease forms, or notices to pay rent, to vacate the premises, or to file a court eviction. If the forms are merely recommended then it may be better to use your own form or to adapt the recommended form, adding improvements where necessary.

OTHER LAWS

You should carefully read your state and local laws that apply to renting property since there are all kinds of strange provisions that you might not ever imagine which were made into laws. In California, for example, the landlord must advise the tenant if the property is located within a mile of property that once was (but is presently not) a military base.

LEASE BASICS

The minimum that a real estate lease should contain to be enforceable is:

- identification of the parties;

- description of the premises;

- clear terms of payment;

- an agreement to rent; and

- a term.

In order to protect against various potential losses, both landlord and tenant are advised to add specific clauses to cover many different situations that may arise during the tenancy. An owner often has most of his life savings in his properties and depends upon a steady cash flow for income or mortgage payments. A tenant will be spending a portion of his or her life at the premises and if things do not go right, that time could be miserable.

Some tenants take care of—and even improve—the property they rent, but far too many cause serious damage to the premises and disappear owing rent. Some landlords look out for their tenant's interests and try to keep them happy; others do not.

For the landlord, a lease can offer these protections:

- locks the tenant in for a set term; and

- provides remedies for actions by tenants.

For the tenant a lease can offer these protections:

- locks the landlord in for a set term;

- assures him that the rent will not be raised during the term; and

- protects his enjoyment of the premises.

LEASE VERSUS RENTAL AGREEMENT

The difference between a lease and a rental agreement is usually that a *lease* is for a set term, such as a year. A *rental agreement* is for a tenancy that may be terminated by either party at any time (usually with reasonable notice).

Since some landlords do not want to be locked into a certain term or rent amount, they sometimes shy away from signing leases. There are agreements being used, some of which are titled "rental agreements," that attempt to lock in a tenant, but which allow the landlord to terminate them at any time. Most of these are not legally enforceable. An agreement in which one party must perform while the other party can get out at any time is not a binding contract. If the landlord can terminate the lease at any time, then the tenant can also terminate the lease at any time, even if the lease says he is bound for a set term.

Similarly, there are leases that state that in the event of litigation the tenant must pay the landlord's attorney's fees. If it does not say that the tenant only pays if he loses, or that the loser pays the winner's attorney's fees, it could be considered unconscionable by a court.

In considering the use of these types of agreements a landlord must weigh the likelihood of a lawsuit with the benefits of using a strong agreement. Most tenants may believe these clauses are enforceable and few tenants have their leases reviewed by an attorney, so most of the time the unenforceable clauses may serve their purpose. (In the few cases that do go to court the landlord would be advised to settle with the tenant and consider it a price to be paid for all the other times the clause worked.)

Tough leases work best with middle class tenants who cannot afford legal advice. The rich can afford lawyers and the poor get free lawyers. The biggest danger for the landlord is having a tenant who qualifies for free legal aid. These lawyers, usually paid for with the landlord's tax dollars, know how to drag on a case for months or even years.

For the landlord who wants to be able to evict an unruly tenant or sell the property without resort to questionable clauses, there are other solutions that can be used in a carefully worded lease.

- The lease should clearly spell out what acts constitute a default under the lease. Strict compliance should be demanded and evictions carried out immediately after a default.

- If a landlord intends to sell a property some time during the term of the lease, he can either have a month-to-month tenancy and risk losing a tenant early, or he can give himself an "option to terminate the lease." Rather than allowing a landlord to terminate at any time, which would make the lease unenforceable, the *option to terminate* could come into effect only if the property were sold. (There is a possibility in some areas that even such an option would make the lease unenforceable against the tenant. To be sure that it would be enforceable it should provide that the landlord could terminate only if he paid some consideration to the tenant. This consideration could be thirty days notice plus $100 credit against rent, or one month's free rent.)

EVICTIONS

In some areas *evictions* are expensive and time-consuming procedures, but in other areas court clerks supply eviction forms and it is relatively fast and simple. Books on how to do an eviction are available in some states. The better ones include do-it-yourself forms and explain each step in the process.

As discussed earlier the landlord should screen the tenants carefully. The landlord should always get a tenant application with a list of several past landlords. Do not ask the present landlord for a reference. He may say the tenant is good just to get rid of him. Ask a previous landlord.

Be careful of tenants who use the name of a friend as a former landlord. Ask the landlord questions about the tenant, such as the amount of the rent, starting and ending dates of the tenancy, who the other tenants in the building were, etc.

In some areas the laws give more rights to tenants who have leases. If this is the case in your area, you can use a rental agreement with no set term. However, you must realize that with a rental agreement the tenants can leave after a month or two and you may lose money on vacancies. This is especially true in areas where rentals are seasonal and in certain months rents are higher.

BASIC LEASE CLAUSES 7

This chapter contains all of the basic clause options used in real estate leases. It offers different versions of most of them, each of which offers different legal rights. You should read each option to see which one best suits your needs.

After choosing from the basic options in this chapter you should go to the residential, commercial, or storage space clauses in the following chapters for the rest of the options for clauses needed in your lease.

For most clauses the different positions of the landlord and tenant are explained. In a few, the position of both parties is the same so just the purpose of the clause is explained.

Whether you are a landlord or tenant you can use this chapter to analyze a lease you are signing to see how each clause affects your rights.

If you are a landlord you can use it to create a lease which best protects your interests.

NOTE: *While many leases use the words lessor and lessee, we have used the terms landlord and tenant to make the book easier to understand.*

Parties, Property, Consideration, Agreement

Purpose

The lease must contain the names of the parties, a description of the property, a recitation of *consideration* (mutual agreements in the lease), and an agreement (*covenant*) to rent. It is best for all parties if there is a clear description of exactly what property is meant to be included in the lease.

Landlord's Position

It is usually in the landlord's interest to have all adult tenants sign the lease. That way they could all be held liable in case of default. If the tenant is a corporation—especially a new corporation—or a trust, then the landlord should require an officer or beneficiary to personally guarantee the lease.

Tenant's Position

If the tenants are a married couple, then it is better if only one of them signs the lease. If both sign the lease then all of their joint property could possibly be subject to the landlord's claim.

Option #1

Landlord:_____   Tenant:_____

_____   _____

_____   _____

Property:_____
__IN CONSIDERATION of the mutual covenants and agreements herein contained, Landlord hereby leases to Tenant and Tenant hereby leases from Landlord the above described property together with any personal property listed on "Schedule A" attached hereto, under the following terms and conditions.

OPTION #2

THIS AGREEMENT is made this ___ day of _____, _____ by and between _____ as Landlord and _____ as Tenant for the rental of property described as_____ together with any personal property listed on "Schedule A" attached hereto.

IN CONSIDERATION of the mutual covenants and agreements herein contained, Landlord hereby leases to Tenant, and Tenant hereby leases from Landlord the above-described property under the following terms and conditions:

NOTE: *If the property is furnished be sure to list all furnishings on a separate "Schedule A." This list should also list previous damage to any of the property, so that it will be clear if any damage was done by this tenant.*

NOTE: *Both options allow you to attach a list of personal property to the lease, which will be included as part of the lease. You can omit the reference to Schedule "A" if there is no additional property leased. The only difference is whether you prefer to list the parties first, or within the text of the lease.*

PAYMENT

PURPOSE

The place and manner of rent payment should be clearly spelled out. In some states a landlord may require that payment must be in cash even if the lease does not say so, but in other states this is not so.

LANDLORD'S POSITION

If a landlord has accepted checks throughout a tenancy, it is possible that he will not be able to suddenly demand cash. In any case, it is best to have it clearly spelled out in the lease. Landlords have had to litigate as far as appeals court to win the issue of whether they could require cash.

TENANT'S POSITION

The tenant does not have a separate position in this clause because rent is solely a landlord benefit.

OPTION #1

PAYMENT. Payments must be received by Landlord on or before the due date at the following address:_____

_____

_____ or such place as designated by Landlord in writing. Tenant understands that this may require early mailing. In the event a check bounces, Landlord may require cash or certified funds.

Option 1 only allows the Landlord to demand rent in cash if the tenant's check bounces.

OPTION #2

PAYMENT OF RENT. Payments must be received by the Landlord on or before the due date at the following address:

_____

or such other place as designated by Landlord in writing. Payments sent through the mail are at Tenant's risk, and Tenant acknowledges that early mailing may be required for rent to be received on time. Landlord reserves the right, at any time, to require that the rent be paid in the form of cash or certified funds.

Option 2 allows the Landlord to require cash rent at any time.

NOTE: *Both options require early mailing of rent to ensure on-time payment. Check your state's laws to see which option is allowed.*

SECURITY DEPOSITS

PURPOSE   There is generally a clause indicating the amount of money a tenant must pay up front. This is for the landlord to hold in case of damage to the premises, or perhaps the tenant leaves without paying rent.

A security deposit is one of the most important things for a landlord to have in a lease. It is the best protection a landlord has against damage to the premises or a default in the lease. In some areas it is common for a landlord to require both a security deposit and a last month's rent deposit. In others, there is just one security deposit that can be used for any type of damages; not just rent.

Tenant would like to get his deposit back at the time he is vacating the premises (See Option 2 under "Surrender of Premises" on page 54.)

Last Month's Rent *plus* Security Deposit

OPTION #1

SECURITY. Tenant shall pay to Landlord the sum of $_____ as last month's rent under this lease, plus $_____ as security deposit.

Security Deposit Only

OPTION #2

SECURITY. Tenant shall pay to Landlord the sum of $_____ as security for the performance of this agreement. Said amount shall not be used as rent.

Forfeiture of Deposit; Additional Damages

OPTION #3

(Same as Option 1 or 2 but add): In the event Tenant terminates the lease prior to its expiration date, said amounts are non-refundable as a charge for Landlord's trouble in finding a new tenant, but Landlord reserves the right to seek additional damages if they exceed the amount of deposits.

NOTE: *Option 3 should allow the landlord to keep the entire security deposit if the tenant breaches the lease by vacating early. However, if the tenant takes the issue to court, a court may find it unenforceable since it allows the landlord to choose the higher of two ways of figuring damages. Wording it this way is much better than the options that say that if a tenant leaves early he forfeits his deposit. (Courts "abhor" a forfeiture and would usually rule against one.)*

Use of Deposit during Tenancy

OPTION #4

(Same as Option 1 or 2 but add): Landlord may use such amounts of the security deposit as are reasonably necessary to remedy Tenant's default in payment of the rent or other terms of this lease, or for legal costs, during or upon termination of the tenancy

NOTE: *Security deposits are strictly regulated in many areas. Some laws require separate bank accounts or the payment of interest to the tenant. You should investigate the rules in your area and comply with them. Some of the above options may not be enforceable in some areas.*

Return of Deposit and Keys Addition

OPTION #5

(Add to any of the above clauses): Security deposit shall be returned to tenant upon return of keys to landlord.

SEVERABILITY

PURPOSE
In case a court finds that one part of the lease is void, unenforceable or unconscionable, this clause prevents the entire lease from being void.

LANDLORD'S POSITION
The landlord usually does not want that one clause to cause the whole lease to be thrown out.

TENANT'S POSITION
Tenant's rights are usually not affected by this clause.

OPTION #1
SEVERABILITY. In the event any section of this agreement shall be held to be invalid all remaining provisions shall remain in full force and effect.

OPTION #2
SEVERABILITY. All provisions in this lease are severable and in the event any of the provisions are ruled by any court of competent jurisdiction to be invalid, the remainder shall continue in full force and effect.

OPTION #3
SEVERABILITY. If any provision of this lease should be or become invalid, such invalidity shall not in any way affect any of the other provisions of this lease which shall continue to remain in full force and effect.

The above three options are different ways of wording this *severability* clause. Which option you use is really a matter of preference, because they essentially say the same thing in a different way. They have similar affects of holding a lease intact.

ATTORNEY'S FEES

PURPOSE
Both parties usually want to be reimbursed for their legal fees if they must go to court to protect their rights.

LANDLORD'S
POSITION
The landlord wants to be reimbursed for his legal fees in the event that he has any trouble with tenant.

TENANT'S
POSITION
The tenant prefers not to pay legal fees unless he is taken to court and loses in court. He would like to have his legal fees paid if he wins in court.

Prevailing Party Gets Fees in All Courts (regarding lease)

OPTION #1
> ATTORNEY'S FEES. In the event of any legal proceedings regarding this agreement, including appellate proceedings, the prevailing party shall be entitled to a reasonable attorney's fee.

Option 1 is usually the one found in leases.

Only Landlord Gets Attorney Fees from Tenant

OPTION #2
> ATTORNEY'S FEES. In the event Landlord must use the services of an attorney to enforce this agreement, Tenant shall pay Landlord's attorney fees.

Prevailing Party Gets Fees Even without Court Action

OPTION #3
> ATTORNEY'S FEES. In the event of any legal proceedings regarding this agreement, including appellate proceedings, the prevailing party shall be entitled to a reasonable attorney's fee. "Legal proceedings" shall include any legal services used prior to commencement of litigation.

NOTE: *The second and third are better for the landlord since it allows attorney's fees even if an attorney merely sends a letter and does not go to court.*

NOTE: *In some areas the winner of any court case would be allowed attorney's fees no matter what the lease says. Therefore there is a chance that the second option might be found unconscionable, since it does not grant the tenant the right to fees even if he wins. Therefore the third alternative might be preferred by a careful landlord.*

Prevailing Party Gets Fees in All Courts
(regarding any action)

OPTION #4

> ATTORNEY'S FEES. In the event of any legal proceedings between the parties hereto, including appellate proceedings, the prevailing party shall be entitled to a reasonable attorney's fee.

Option 4 is like Option 1 but it covers any suits between the parties, even if they are not related to the lease. This would usually be better for the tenant since the tenant would be more likely to have a claim unrelated to the lease, such as a claim for injuries on the premises.

Each Party Pays Own Fees

OPTION #5

> ATTORNEY'S FEES. In the event of a dispute between the parties hereto, each agrees to pay his or her own attorney fees.

NOTE: *Because a judgment can be enforced against a tenant for up to twenty years in some areas (with interest) it is good to obtain one in any litigation against a tenant. Even the most judgment-proof (unable to collect from) tenant might get an inheritance or win the lottery some day. However, if a landlord is more concerned with countersuits by tenants with legal aid lawyers, he might consider a option stating that each party will pay their own attorney's fees. In some states this might be overruled by a statute or judge, but in others it could save money and avoid litigation.*

JURY WAIVER

PURPOSE

A jury waiver clause allows for a trial without a jury. Only a judge presides.

LANDLORD'S
POSITION

While a lawsuit is taking place between a landlord and tenant, the tenant is often using the property rent-free. Since jury trials usually take longer than trials before a judge, tenants often request them just to buy time. Also, some believe that juries more often side with tenants. Therefore the *waiver* of a jury trial is in the landlord's interest.

TENANT'S
POSITION

Tenants would prefer this clause not be in the lease because they would like the option of having a jury trial.

Waiver Regarding Lease

OPTION #1

JURY WAIVER. Both Landlord and Tenant hereby waive trial by jury in any action arising out of this agreement.

Waiver Including Any Issue over Property

OPTION #2

JURY WAIVER. Both Landlord and Tenant hereby waive trial by jury in any action arising out of this agreement or tenant's use of the premises.

NOTE: *In some areas the jury waiver clause may be unenforceable and some judges may even consider it unconscionable. Option 2 is even stronger since it waives a jury trial in claims even unrelated to the lease (such as an injury by the tenant) but it has even more risk of being unenforceable or unconscionable.*

WAIVER

PURPOSE This clause makes it clear that allowing a tenant to do something once does not mean it can happen again.

LANDLORD'S POSITION If the landlord lets a tenant get away with something once, the tenant may be able to legally do it again.

TENANT'S POSITION A tenant prefers to have the same rights as the landlord.

Clause Protecting Landlord

OPTION #1

WAIVER. Any failure by Landlord to exercise any rights under this agreement shall not constitute a waiver of Landlord's rights.

Clause Protecting Both Parties

OPTION #2

WAIVER. Any failure by a party under this agreement to exercise any rights under this agreement shall not constitute a waiver of that party's rights.

Option 2 allows the same rights to both parties, and is considered more fair by courts.

Alternative Clause Protecting Landlord
(allows waiver of specific provisions)

OPTION #3

WAIVER. If Landlord should waive any provision of this lease, it shall not be construed as a waiver of a further breach of such provisions.

Clause Protecting Landlord (allows multiple waivers)

OPTION #4

WAIVER. One or more waivers of any covenant or condition by the Landlord shall not be construed as a waiver of a further breach of the same covenant or condition.

ABANDONMENT

PURPOSE

In the event the tenant leaves the property and removes his or her possessions before the lease ends, this clause allows the landlord some choices.

LANDLORD'S
POSITION

The landlord wants to quickly re-rent premises if the tenant disappears. Because there can be a dispute as to whether or not the property was actually *abandoned* by the tenant, the landlord may want a clear definition of abandonment. However, this definition might be overruled by another definition provided in state or local laws.

TENANT'S
POSITION

The tenant would prefer that there is a clear definition of what abandonment is, such as in Options 2 and 3.

Simple Clause

OPTION #1

ABANDONMENT. In the event Tenant abandons the property prior to the expiration of this lease, Landlord may relet the premises and hold Tenant liable for any costs, lost rent or damage to the premises. Landlord may dispose of any personal property abandoned by Tenant.

Simple Clause plus Abandonment Definition

OPTION #2

ABANDONMENT. In the event Tenant abandons the property prior to the expiration of this lease, Landlord may relet the premises and hold Tenant liable for any costs, lost rent or damage to the premises. Landlord may dispose of any personal property abandoned by Tenant. Abandonment shall be deemed to be removal of most of Tenant's possessions from the property or being absent from the property for fifteen days without notice to landlord.

Option 2 gives the landlord a clear definition of abandonment.

Clause with Expanded Rights for Landlord

OPTION #3

ABANDONMENT. In the event Tenant abandons the property prior to the expiration of this lease, Landlord may (1) retake the premises for the account of the Tenant and hold Tenant liable for the difference in any rent received, (2) retake the premises for Landlord's own account and relieve Tenant of further liability, or (3) do nothing and hold Tenant liable for the rent. Landlord may dispose of any personal property abandoned by Tenant. Abandonment shall be deemed to be removal of most of Tenant's possessions from the property or being absent from the property for fifteen days without notice to Landlord.

Clause with Detailed Landlord Rights
(plus right of reentry)

OPTION #4

ABANDONMENT. If at any time during the term of this lease Tenant abandons the premises or any part thereof, Landlord may, at his option, obtain possession of the premises in the manner provided by law, and without becoming liable to Tenant for damages or for any payment of any kind whatever. Landlord may, at his discretion, as agent for Tenant, relet the premises, or any part thereof, for the whole or any part of the then unexpired term, and may receive and collect all rent payable by virtue of such reletting, and at Landlord's option, hold Tenant liable for any difference between the rent that would have been payable under this lease during the balance of the unexpired term, if this lease had continued in force, and the net rent for such period realized by Landlord by means of such reletting. If Landlord's right of reentry is exercised following abandonment of the premises by Tenant, then Landlord may consider any personal property belonging to Tenant and left on the premises to also have been abandoned, in which case Landlord may dispose of all such personal property in any manner Landlord shall deem proper and is hereby relieved of all liability for doing so.

Options 3 and 4 give the landlord more choices, but check local law limitations. (In commercial leases there would usually not be local laws that would overrule the clauses.)

NOTE: *Some areas have laws regarding personal property abandoned by tenants and in some cases notice of abandoned property must be placed in the newspaper. Check your local laws.*

SUBORDINATION

PURPOSE

This clause allows the landlord to refinance the property.

The landlord may have trouble refinancing the property unless the tenants *subordinate* their leasehold interest in the property to the financing. (This means that the tenants agree that the lender has a higher right to the property than the tenants.)

LANDLORD'S
POSITION

The risk to the tenant is that if the bank forecloses, then the lease will no longer be in effect. In both residential and commercial tenancies this could mean either termination of the tenancy or higher rent. In a soft rental market the landlord may be glad to have the tenant stay at the same rent, but in a commercial tenancy where the tenant has thousands of dollars invested in the business premises the lender could use this to force the rent higher.

TENANT'S
POSITION

The tenant would prefer not to subordinate his lease to the lender because then the lender could remove him if there is a foreclosure. However, in most cases (unless the rent is low) the lender would prefer for him to stay and pay rent. So in most cases this is not a big issue. The best situation for the tenant would be to not have this clause in the lease.

Tenant Agrees to Sign Subordination Documents

OPTION #1

> SUBORDINATION. Tenant's interest in the premises shall be subordinate to any encumbrances now on or hereafter placed on the premises, to any advances made under such encumbrances, and to any extensions or renewals thereof. Tenant agrees to sign any documents indicating such subordination which may be required by lenders.

NOTE: *Option 1 is the stronger of the two options here, giving the landlord the right to obtain new financing and requiring the tenant to sign necessary documents.*

No Tenant Signature Required

OPTION #2

> SUBORDINATION. This lease and Tenant's interest hereunder are and shall be subordinated to any liens or encumbrances now or hereafter placed on the premises by Landlord, all advances made under any such liens or encumbrances, the interest payable on any such liens or encumbrances, and any and all renewals or extensions of such liens or encumbrances.

The tenant would prefer Option 2 because a new, larger mortgage would bring greater risk of default that could result in tenant's lease being terminated.

SURRENDER OF PREMISES

PURPOSE
This clause lays out how the property is to be returned after renting.

LANDLORD'S
POSITION
The landlord wants to insure that the tenant understands that the premises must be returned (*surrendered*) properly in a clean condition. The landlord also wants to be sure to get all the keys back. (Since one never knows if the tenant made more duplicate keys it is best to change the locks whenever a tenant leaves.)

TENANT'S
POSITION
One problem for tenants is that some landlords expect that the tenant is responsible for returning the premises to its original condition. In most areas the tenant is not responsible for normal wear and tear. The tenant should not leave the premises dirty or damaged, but could not be held liable for the wear related to the time the tenant occupied the premises. From the tenant's point of view it is best to spell this out in the lease, but even if it is not spelled out this will usually be the situation. Tenant would also like to have his deposit returned at the time of surrender.

Surrender with No Landlord Obligation

OPTION #1
> SURRENDER OF PREMISES. At the expiration of the term of this lease, Tenant shall immediately surrender possession of the premises in as good condition as at the start of this lease. The Tenant shall turn over to Landlord all keys to the premises, including keys made by Tenant or Tenant's agents.

Option 1 is best for the landlord

Surrender with Landlord Obligation—Return of Deposit

OPTION #2
> SURRENDER OF PREMISES. At the expiration of the term of this lease, Tenant shall surrender possession of the premises in clean and undamaged condition, normal wear and tear excepted. Upon return of Tenant's security deposit Tenant shall turn over to Landlord all keys to the premises, including keys made by Tenant or Tenant's agents.

Option 2 is best for the tenant because Option 2 requires the landlord to give back the deposit at the time the keys are returned.

ALTERATIONS AND IMPROVEMENTS

PURPOSE
This clause sets the standards by which a tenant can change the rented property with things like paint and fixtures.

LANDLORD'S POSITION
The landlord does not want tenants to alter the premises or to use unusual paint colors on the premises. (Many a landlord has found purple, black or burnt umber rooms upon return of the premises.) The landlord also does not want the tenant modifying the electrical or plumbing systems, which could cause damage to the property or to other tenants spaces.

TENANT'S POSITION
The tenant wants flexibility to modify the premises, and if the modifications improve the value of the property or the tenant agrees to return the premises to its original state, there should be no objection from the landlord.

No Alterations without Landlord's Consent

OPTION #1
ALTERATIONS & IMPROVEMENTS. Tenant shall make no alterations or improvements to the premises (including paint) without the written consent of the Landlord and any such alterations or improvements shall become the property of the Landlord unless otherwise agreed in writing.

Minor Alterations Allowed

OPTION #2
ALTERATIONS & IMPROVEMENTS. Tenant may make minor alterations to the premises (such as paint, wallpaper, light fixtures) to suit Tenant's needs.

The following options are more appropriate for commercial leases.

Commercial Alterations Clause

OPTION #3

ALTERATIONS & IMPROVEMENTS. Tenant shall make no alterations to the buildings on the premises or construct any building improvements on the premises without the prior written consent of Landlord. All alterations, changes, and improvement built, constructed, or placed on the premises by Tenant, with the exception of fixtures removable without damage to the premises and movable personal property, shall, unless otherwise provided by written agreement between Landlord and Tenant, be the property of Landlord and remain on the premises at the expiration or sooner termination of this lease.

Commercial Alterations Clause—Landlord Controls Work

OPTION #4

ALTERATIONS & IMPROVEMENTS. Tenant shall make no alterations, decoration, additions or improvements in or to the premises without Landlord's prior written consent and then only by contractors or mechanics approved by Landlord. All such work shall be done at such times and in such manner as Landlord may from time to time designate. All alterations, additions or improvements upon the premises, made by either party shall become the property of Landlord, and shall remain upon, and be surrendered with the premises at the termination of this lease. Any mechanic's lien filed against the premises, or the building, for work claimed to have been done for Tenant, shall be discharged by Tenant within ten days thereafter at Tenant's expenses by filing a bond as required by law.

RECORDING

PURPOSE
: Most leases need to establish whether recording of leases is allowed.

LANDLORD'S POSITION
: Landlords want to be sure the lease is not *recorded* in the public records, since it would be a *cloud* on his title to the property.

TENANT'S POSITION
: The tenant usually does not need to record the lease unless it is a long-term commercial lease.

> RECORDING. This lease shall not be recorded in any public records.

NOTE: *In many areas a document cannot be recorded unless it is notarized. Therefore a landlord should not allow his or her signature to be notarized.*

ACCESS

PURPOSE
This clause sets out what rights a landlord has to go into the rented property.

LANDLORD'S
POSITION
In some states the laws give the landlord the right to enter the premises for such things as inspection, repairs, or showing them to prospective tenants or purchasers. (This is called the *right of access*.)In other areas the landlord has no right to enter the premises unless such a right is reserved in the lease. In any case it is best for both parties if the right of the landlord is spelled out clearly in the lease. This way there can be no misunderstanding.

TENANT'S
POSITION
The tenant prefers that the access be only at reasonable times and that he or she be given prior notice.

Unlimited Access

OPTION #1
ACCESS. Landlord reserves the right to enter the premises, for the purpose of inspection, repair, or showing to prospective tenants or purchasers.

Access Only with Notice

OPTION #2
ACCESS. Landlord reserves the right to enter the premises, upon giving reasonable notice, for the purpose of inspection, repair, or showing to prospective tenants or purchasers.

Access Only at Reasonable Times

OPTION #3
ACCESS. Landlord reserves the right to enter the premises, at reasonable hours, for the purpose of inspection, repair, or showing to prospective tenants or purchasers.

Access Only at Reasonable Times—Signs Allowed

OPTION #4

ACCESS. Landlord reserves the right to enter the premises, at reasonable hours, for the purpose of inspection, repair, or showing to prospective tenants or purchasers. Landlord may place "For Sale" or "For Rent" signs on the premises.

Additional Notice (add to any of above Options 1-4)

OPTION #5

Landlord shall give tenant at least 24 hours notice of access to the premises except in the event of an emergency.

ENTIRE AGREEMENT

PURPOSE

It is in both parties' best interest to have any agreements between them be spelled out in writing to avoid false accusations.

Change Lease with One Party's Signature

OPTION #1

ENTIRE AGREEMENT. This lease constitutes the entire agreement between the parties and may not be modified except in writing.

Change Lease with Both Parties' Signatures

OPTION #2

ENTIRE AGREEMENT. This lease constitutes the entire agreement between the parties and may not be modified except in writing signed by both parties.

NOTE: *It is often enough that one party sign any written modification. For example, if the landlord wrote a letter to the tenant saying that it was okay to paint the kitchen, the letter probably would not have to be signed by the tenant.*

LOCKS

PURPOSE

This clause dictates the installation of locks.

LANDLORD'S
POSITION

The landlord wants to always have a key to the property so that he can get in for emergencies and in the event the tenant disappears.

TENANT'S
POSITION

The tenant usually cannot keep the landlord from having a key to the premises, but might like to change the locks in case the last tenant kept a set of keys. For extra protection the tenant should insist on permission to add a deadbolt lock, if one is not provided, on each exterior door.

No Lock Changes Allowed

OPTION #1

LOCKS. No locks shall be installed without Landlord's written permission and Landlord shall be given a key to each lock installed by Tenant.

Most landlords prefer to use Option 1 because they do not want tenants drilling holes in the doors or otherwise altering the premises. However, an option like this caused a court to hold a landlord liable when a tenant was raped by a person who broke into the premises.

Lock Change Allowed-Give Key to Landlord

OPTION #2

LOCKS. If Tenant adds to or changes the locks on the premises, Landlord shall be given copies of the keys. Landlord shall at all times have keys for access to the premises in case of emergencies.

Option 2 might help avoid liability. You may leave off the reference to emergencies in Option 2.

RESIDENTIAL LEASE CLAUSES 8

This chapter contains various provisions applicable to residential leases. Since residential tenancies are much more strictly regulated than commercial tenancies, you should carefully check your state and local laws to be sure that any lease you use complies.

This chapter relates the differences between the landlord's position and the tenant's position wherever possible as in Chapter 7. (see page 37.)

TERM

PURPOSE

The lease can be for a set *term* such as a year, or for renewable terms of a month or a week each. If there is a set term the document is properly called a *lease*; if it is of indefinite duration then the document would be called a *rental agreement*. In any case, the term should be clear, including the starting and ending date.

Fixed-Term

OPTION #1

TERM. This lease shall be for a term of _____ beginning on _____, _____ and ending _____, _____.

Month-to-Month

OPTION #2

TERM. The term of this agreement shall begin on _____, _____ and continues thereafter as a month-to-month tenancy until terminated by either party.

Month-to-Month—Certified Mail Termination

OPTION #3

TERM. The term of this agreement shall begin on _____, _____ and continues thereafter as a month-to-month tenancy until terminated by either party. Notice of termination must be given by certified mail at least _____ days prior to the date of termination.

Month-to-Month—30 Days Notice

OPTION #4

> TERM. This rental agreement shall be for a month-to-month tenancy which may be cancelled by either party upon giving notice to the other party at least 30 days prior to the end of the month.

NOTE: *Some states have laws stating that if no notice is given the lease is assumed to renew. Others have laws that state the opposite—the lease is assumed to terminate unless renewal is agreed upon by the parties. You should get in touch with your landlord or tenant well in advance of the expiration to discuss whether the lease will be renewed and whether there will be any changes.*

RENT

PURPOSE

The amount of rent and the due date should be clear and the inclusion of additional fees can avoid problems. Late fees and other such fees should be reasonable; otherwise a court may say they are void. The following are two ways of laying out the same information. There is no other difference between them.

OPTION #1

RENT. The rent shall be $_____ per _____ and shall be due on or before the _____ day of each _____ without demand. In the event the full amount of rent is not received on the due date, a late fee of $____ shall be due. In the event a check is returned unpaid or an eviction notice must be posted, Tenant agrees to pay a $_____ charge.

OPTION #2

RENT. The rent shall be $_____ per _____ and shall be due on or before _____ without demand. In the event the full amount of rent is not received on the due date, then the following charges shall be due:

If paid more than ___ days late	$_____
If check is returned unpaid	$_____
If legal notice must be posted	$_____

NOTE: *See the next page for an alternative Rent paragraph—one offering a discount for early payment of the rent.*

Knox Learning Center
SW Tech Library Services
1800 Bronson Boulevard
Fennimore, WI 53809

DISCOUNTED RENT

PURPOSE   One way to insure that rent is on time and that the tenant complies with the lease is to offer a *discount* on the rent. Suppose that you need $450 rent from a property. If you can reasonably say that there are other houses like it renting for $500, tell the tenant the rent is really $500, but he or she will get a $50 discount for paying rent one day early and for maintaining the premises.

NOTE: *A discount looks much better to a tenant and to a judge than a late penalty. However, a late fee may also be used with a discount. Be careful not to make it too harsh or a court may throw out the lease.*

Early Payment Discount

OPTION #1

RENT. The rent shall be $_____ per _____ and shall be due on or before _____ day of each _____ without demand. In the event payment is received by Landlord prior to this day, and if Tenant is in compliance with all other terms of this agreement, then there shall be a discount of $_____ from the rent due.

Early Payment Discount *plus* Late Payment Penalties

OPTION #2

RENT. The rent shall be $_____ per _____ and shall be due on or before _____ day of each _____ without demand. In the event payment is received by Landlord prior to this day, and if Tenant is in compliance with all other terms of this agreement, then there shall be a discount of $_____ from the rent due. In the event the full amount of rent is not received within _____ days of due date, an additional fee of $_____ shall be due. In the event a check bounces, or if an eviction notice is posted by Landlord, Tenant shall pay an additional $_____ fee.

DEFAULT

PURPOSE

If the tenant *defaults* in any way under the lease, the landlord wants to quickly force the tenant to cure the default or to vacate the premises.

LANDLORD'S POSITION

The landlord should not agree to sending notices by certified mail because of the delay in delivery and the possibility that the tenant will refuse to accept the certified mail. If the tenant refuses to accept a certified letter the landlord has still fulfilled his obligation of giving notice. The post office usually gives the recipient two chances to claim the letter and it may take ten days to two weeks for the letter to come back.

TENANT'S POSITION

Because it is possible for a landlord to say that a notice was given when it was not, the tenant would prefer that all notices be sent by certified mail.

Simple Clause

OPTION #1

DEFAULT. In the event Tenant defaults under any term of this lease, Landlord may recover possession as provided by law and seek monetary damages.

Clause Giving Landlord Options for Tenant's Default

OPTION #2

DEFAULT. In the event that Tenant fails to pay the rent due, or otherwise defaults under the terms of this lease, Landlord may give notice to correct such breach or may terminate this lease as provided by law, and retake possession. Landlord may seek monetary damages for any breach of this lease.

Simple Clause—Equal Remedies for Both Parties

OPTION #3

DEFAULT. In the event that either party defaults under this lease, the other party may give notice to correct such breach or may terminate this lease by giving 15 days notice by certified mail.

NOTE: *Each state or city may have different requirements for terminating a lease. Often there are specific rules for what notices must be given. If you do not use the exact wording required by some states, you lose all rights. You should become familiar with the rules in your area.*

UTILITIES

PURPOSE
The agreement should clearly spell out who pays for what utilities on the premises.

Simple Clause

OPTION #1

UTILITIES. Tenant agrees to pay all utility charges on the property except: _____.

In some cases a landlord will put the utilities in his own name if a tenant does not have the deposit money. This is risky because a landlord may get stuck with a big bill. (Tenants have been known to let the water run continuously or to leave the air conditioning on with the windows open once there is a disagreement with the landlord.) In many areas landlords may not shut off utilities if a tenant does not pay rent. But a landlord should not have to pay a tenant's utility bills if they are paid separately from rent. The following clause may help, but check local law.

Clause with Right to Switch Account to Tenant

OPTION #2

UTILITIES. Tenant agrees to pay all utility charges on the property except: _____.
In the event Tenant is unable to have utilities put in Tenant's name, Landlord may have them temporarily put in Landlord's name until such time as Tenant is able to have them switched over. In the event Tenant fails to pay the amount of the utilities to Landlord, Landlord may instruct utility company to remove landlord's name from the account. Tenant shall then be responsible for having utilities placed in his own name.

NOTE: *The above clause is an attempt to get around the issue of "shutting off" the utilities by stating that the responsibility is shifted to the tenant. However, it is possible that in the event of a lawsuit a judge would rule that the landlord shut off the utilities by having his name taken off the account, and therefore had violated the law.*

Clause with No Requirement for Landlord to Pay

OPTION #3

> UTILITIES. Tenant agrees to pay all utility charges on the property except: _____.
> In the event Tenant is unable to have utilities put in Tenant's name, Landlord may have them temporarily put in Landlord's name until such time as Tenant is able to have them switched over to Tenant's name. Landlord shall forward to the utility companies amounts paid by Tenant but shall have no responsibility to use Landlord's own funds toward Tenant's utilities.

The problem with the approach in Option 3 is that a court may still interpret this action as it shutting off the utilities and the landlord might get a bad credit rating by not paying the bill. A more creative approach would be to have the utilities put in the name of a third party who is not named on the lease, such as a spouse, child or sibling of the landlord. A separate agreement could be drawn up between the tenant and the third party for payment of the utilities. This way the landlord would not be legally involved if the utilities were shut off. Of course a misguided judge might still rule against the landlord, but he or she would have to ignore the legal framework of the transaction. (To the best of the author's knowledge this arrangement has not been tested in court. If any readers of this book use this arrangement successfully in court, kindly inform the author by writing care of the publisher.)

Landlords who have utilities in their names and anticipate possible problems with tenants should consult a local landlord/tenant attorney to see what local courts allow.

In some cases, utility bills must be prorated between landlord and tenant or among tenants. In such cases language like this should be used:

Clause Where Tenant Pays Percentage of Bills

OPTION #4

> UTILITIES. Tenant agrees to pay _____% of the _____ _____ bills on the premises within five days of receipt from Landlord.

MAINTENANCE

PURPOSE
The lease should clearly spell out who is responsible for what maintenance on the premises.

LANDLORD'S POSITION
In some cases, such as apartment buildings, the landlord usually does most maintenance. In other cases, such as single family homes, tenants can be put in charge of all maintenance.

By making the tenant responsible for maintaining the property the landlord can avoid both the headaches of management and the liability for negligent maintenance. Since rents can vary greatly, you can mention that the regular rent is a higher amount but that there is a discount if the tenant handles the maintenance.

If a landlord is responsible for maintenance, then the landlord is liable if anyone is injured due to lack of maintenance. (One landlord was liable for $750,000.00 for not fixing a water heater for three days when a woman spilled boiling water on her grandson.) Therefore, in most cases it is advantageous to make the responsibility of maintenance the duty of the tenant.

However, because tenants do not have a personal interest in the property they may neglect the maintenance to save money. A minor problem that is ignored may escalate into an expensive one; a tenant may neglect to change a 50¢ washer and let leaking water cause $1000 damage to a floor.

TENANT'S POSITION
It is important for the tenant to read this clause and be sure that he understands exactly what he is responsible for. If he is responsible for much of the maintenance then the rent should be adjusted accordingly. If the building is old the tenant should be aware that maintenance may be expensive and if it is neglected, resulting in further damage to the property he could be liable.

The following options offer variations as to who handles different amounts of maintenance.

Tenant Does All Maintenance for Reduced Rent

OPTION #1

MAINTENANCE. Tenant has examined the property, acknowledges it to be in good repair, and in consideration of the reduced rent agrees to be responsible for and to promptly complete all maintenance to the premises.

Tenant Does All Maintenance or Reimburses Landlord

OPTION #2

MAINTENANCE. Tenant has examined the property, and in consideration of the agreed rent agrees to be responsible for and to promptly complete all maintenance to the premises. In the event Tenant fails to maintain the premises after notice by Landlord, Landlord may have the maintenance done and shall be reimbursed by Tenant for the actual costs plus $50 for his trouble.

Tenant Does Minor Maintenance—Up to Dollar Amount

OPTION #3

MAINTENANCE. Tenant has examined the property, acknowledges it to be in good repair and agrees to maintain the premises in its present condition including repairs of up to $_____ per incident. Landlord shall only be responsible for major repairs such as roof or appliance repairs of over $_____.

Landlord Does Most Maintenance

OPTION #4

MAINTENANCE. Tenant has examined the property, acknowledges it to be in good repair and agrees to inform Landlord promptly of any maintenance problems. Tenant agrees to keep the premises in clean and sanitary condition. In the event damage has been done by Tenant or Tenant's guests, either intentionally or negligently, Tenant shall pay for such repairs within ten days.

Landlord Does All Maintenance

OPTION #5

MAINTENANCE. Landlord agrees to maintain the premises in compliance with applicable housing and health codes. Tenant agrees to promptly report any maintenance problems to Landlord. In the event damage has been done by Tenant or Tenant's guests, either intentionally or negligently, Tenant shall pay for such repairs within ten days.

NOTE: *In some areas landlords must provide maintenance and cannot put the duty on the tenant. In some areas landlords must provide maintenance for apartment buildings, but single family homes and duplexes can be maintained by tenants.*

In some cases the landlord might want to give one tenant the duty to do maintenance of the common areas in exchange for reduced rent. Because the tenant is at the property daily it would be easier for him than for a landlord who had to make a long trip to do it.

USE

PURPOSE · This clause sets out the parameters of using the rental property.

LANDLORD'S POSITION · The landlord does not want the premises used for any dangerous or illegal activities such as prostitution, drug dealing, or bomb making, which could cause insurance rates to rise or even result in liability for the landlord.

TENANT'S POSITION · Because many people operate home businesses, the tenant may not want to lose this opportunity. If the business is not a bother to the neighbors this should not be a problem to the landlord. In many areas home businesses violate *zoning* or subdivision laws. However, for businesses that consist mainly of a computer and a telephone and no nuisance to neighbors, the laws are usually not enforceable and may even be unconstitutional. Many areas are changing their laws to allow such businesses.

Residential Use Only

OPTION #1

USE. Tenant agrees to use the premises for residential purposes only and not for any illegal purpose or any purpose which will increase the rate of insurance. Tenant further agrees not to violate any zoning laws or subdivision restrictions or to engage in any activity which would injure the premises or constitute a nuisance to the neighbors or Landlord.

Leave Commercial Use Open

OPTION #2

USE. Tenant agrees not to use the premises for any illegal purpose or any purpose which will increase the rate of insurance or to violate any zoning laws or subdivision restrictions. Tenant further agrees not to engage in any activity which would injure the premises or constitute a nuisance to the neighbors or Landlord.

ASSIGNMENT

PURPOSE

This clause explains whether assignment or subleasing are allowed. An *assignment* is where the tenant turns over all of his or her interest in the lease to a new party. The new party takes the place of the tenant and pays rent directly to the landlord. A *sublease* means that the tenant acts as a landlord and re-leases the property to a new tenant. The new tenant pays the rent to the old tenant who forwards it to the landlord. In some cases the tenant can charge a higher rent to the sub-tenant and keep the difference.

LANDLORD'S POSITION

The landlord does not want the tenant to assign the lease to another party unless the landlord can approve the credit and character of the new tenant.

The long standing rule of law has been that a landlord could refuse to accept an assignment for good reason or for no reason. However, the new view, which has been accepted by more and more states, is that the landlord can only reject the new tenant for good reason, such as bad credit.

If there is no clause in the lease governing assignments or subleases, the right would be governed by state law. In some states the tenant has the right to assign the lease unless the lease states otherwise. In other states the tenant has no right to assign the lease unless such right is included in the lease. If you think the other party will object to your clause, and state law is on your side, you may wish to avoid mentioning the issue.

TENANT'S POSITION

If the tenant thinks that he or she may need to vacate the premises early, such as for a home purchase or job transfer, then the right to assign the lease or sublet the property would be important. If the possibility is known at the beginning of the tenancy the tenant should discuss it with the landlord and try to negotiate a right of assignment.

No Assignment Allowed

OPTION #1

> ASSIGNMENT. Tenant may not assign this lease or sublet any part of the premises without Landlord's written consent, which consent shall be at Landlord's sole discretion.

No Unreasonable Assignment—Landlord's Consent

OPTION #2

> ASSIGNMENT. Tenant may not assign this lease or sublet any part of the premises without Landlord's consent in writing, which consent will not be unreasonably withheld.

Assignment Allowed

OPTION #3

> ASSIGNMENT. Tenant reserves the right to assign Tenant's interest in this lease or to sublease the premises.

Assignment Allowed—Tenant Released from Liability

OPTION #4

> ASSIGNMENT. Tenant reserves the right to assign Tenant's interest in this lease or to sublease the premises. In the event of assignment of Tenant's interest, Tenant shall be relieved of liability under this lease and landlord shall look to the assignee for payment.

ASSIGNING THE LEASE

If a lease is being assigned by one tenant to another, an ASSIGNMENT OF LEASE form should be used. The landlord should be a party to this assignment to protect the tenants from liability or eviction. The landlord can consent with or without releasing the original tenant from the obligations of the lease.

An ASSIGNMENT OF LEASE form is included in Appendix B, which allows the landlord either option. (see form 12, p. 192.)

CONDOMINIUM

PURPOSE

This clause establishes that condominium association rules must be followed. Also, the lease should spell out here who is responsible for maintenance fees and who will pay the lease approval fee, if any.

LANDLORD'S
POSITION

If the property is a condominium, the landlord must be sure that the tenant does not violate any of the rules or requirements of the condominiums, or the landlord may have to pay damages to the association.

TENANT'S
POSITION

A person considering renting a condominium unit should obtain and read a copy of the "declaration of condominium" and any other rules and regulations prior to entering into the lease. These should be available from the landlord or from the condominium association. Otherwise you should be able to view them in the public records office of the county in which the property is located.

NOTE: *Some condominiums have very strict rules, such as forbidding the parking of trucks and recreational vehicles on the property, forbidding pets over a certain size, or requiring curtains be of a certain color. If you drive a pickup truck instead of a car you may need to find another place to rent.*

If a tenant has agreed to pay maintenance fees as part of the lease, he should be sure that the lease does not make him responsible for assessments as well. *Assessments* could include one-time charges for roof replacement or painting the building.

Tenant Pays Approval Fees

OPTION #1

CONDOMINIUM. In the event the premises are a condominium unit, Tenant agrees to abide by all applicable rules and regulations. Maintenance and recreation fees are to be paid by _____ _____. This lease is subject to the approval of the condominium association and Tenant agrees to pay any fee necessary for such approval.

Landlord Pays Approval Fees

OPTION #2

CONDOMINIUM. In the event the premises are a condominium unit, Tenant agrees to abide by all applicable rules and regulations. Maintenance and recreation fees are to be paid by _____ _____. This lease is subject to the approval of the condominium association and Landlord agrees to pay any fee necessary for such approval.

LAWN

PURPOSE

This clause should clearly set out who is responsible for lawn maintenance.

LANDLORD'S
POSITION

In apartment buildings or owner-occupied buildings the landlord usually takes care of the lawn and yard maintenance. But, when a tenant rents a single family residence the tenant is usually responsible for it. Either because it is too much work, or because water may be costly, tenants occasionally ignore yard maintenance, which can result in a major expense for resodding. To avoid this possibility, when the tenant has the duty of maintaining the yard, it should be spelled out clearly in the lease.

TENANT'S
POSITION

The tenant would not want to be liable for any damage to the lawn which he did not cause, such as from drought.

OPTION #1

> LAWN. Tenant shall be responsible for maintaining the lawn and shrubbery on the premises at Tenant's expense and for any damages caused by his neglect or abuse thereof.

OPTION #2

> (add to above clause): Tenant shall not be held liable for any damage beyond his control such as from disease or drought.

LIABILITY

PURPOSE

This clause outlines the extent to which each party is responsible for things like damage, loss, injury, and theft.

LANDLORD'S
POSITION

In most areas the landlord cannot avoid *liability* for his own *negligence* through a clause in the lease. However, the landlord should not be responsible for injuries to the tenant or his guests that are not caused by his actions.

Most states have laws covering landlord liability, so the following options might not hold up in all states. (Option 2 should hold up better since it does not limit the liability of the landlord for his own acts—only for the acts of others. This might help in a case where a tenant was responsible for maintenance and a guest was injured due to negligence by tenant.)

Some states have laws stating that any clause in a lease that limits a landlord's liability is void. However, if instead of limiting the landlord's liability the lease included a clause stating that the tenant was responsible for maintenance of the premises, this may have the same effect of limiting the landlord's liability. This is because the liability for failing to maintain the property falls on the party who is responsible for maintaining it. If the landlord does not have the responsibility of maintenance, then he should not be liable if someone is injured due to lack of proper maintenance. Unfortunately, courts sometimes ignore these rules.

TENANT'S
POSITION

The tenant would prefer not to hold harmless the landlord because this means that the tenant would be responsible to defend the landlord if he were sued. In all cases a tenant should have his own liability insurance in case a guest is hurt.

Landlord Not Liable—Tenant Insured

OPTION #1

> LIABILITY. Tenant agrees to hold Landlord harmless from any and all claims for damages that occur on the premises, and to be solely responsible for insuring his own possessions on the premises.

Landlord Liable Only for His Actions—Tenant Insurance

OPTION #2

> LIABILITY. Landlord shall not be liable for any loss or injury on the premises not caused by Landlord. Tenant agrees to be responsible for insurance of his own property if desired.

PETS

PURPOSE

This clause governs whether pets are allowed, which pets, and whether an extra deposit is required.

LANDLORD'S
POSITION

New federal laws forbid discrimination against people with children, but so far landlords can still discriminate against pets. (Do not be surprised if this changes.) One exception is dogs and other animals that aid people with disabilities. Under the 1988 amendment to the Civil Rights Act a landlord might get sued for refusing to rent to a person who needed such an animal.

Because pets can cause extensive damage to property and leave lasting odors, landlords often want to forbid them or require additional deposits. In some cases landlords charge additional rent or make the pet deposit nonrefundable due to the extra wear and tear caused by pets.

TENANT'S
POSITION

Some tenants would like the option to have a pet. In some neighborhoods a dog may be useful for security. Landlords who have not had bad experiences with tenant's pets might agree to Option 4. Option 5 may be pushing it.

Specify Pet and Deposit—Landlord Can Revoke

OPTION #1

> PETS. No pets shall be allowed on the premises except:
> _____ and there shall be a nonre-
> fundable $_____ pet deposit. Landlord reserves
> the right to revoke consent if pet becomes a nuisance.

Tenant's Protection

OPTION #1A

> In the event Landlord revokes consent, Tenant may terminate this lease.

Since a tenant would not want to give up a pet after it has become a member of the family, the tenant would want the above added to Option 1

No Pets without Landlord Consent and New Agreement

OPTION #2

PETS. No pets shall be allowed on the premises without the written consent of Landlord. Landlord may charge additional rent and additional security deposit if pets are kept on the premises and Tenant shall be responsible for all damages resulting from said pet. Landlord reserves the right to revoke consent if pet is determined to be a nuisance.

Specify Pet and Deposit

OPTION #3

PETS. No pets shall be allowed on the premises except: _____ and there shall be a nonrefundable $_____ pet deposit.

Any Two Pets Allowed

OPTION #4

PETS. Tenant shall have no more than two pets on the premises.

Only Two Pets—Litters Accounted For

OPTION #5

PETS. Tenant shall have no more than two pets on the premises unless said pets have a litter in which case all such offspring of the pets shall be sold within a reasonable time after weaning.

OCCUPANCY

PURPOSE

This clause sets out in general how many persons will be living on the premises.

LANDLORD'S
POSITION

The landlord does not want additional parties moving into the premises because it may violate zoning or condominium rules or may put an excessive burden on the sewer or utility systems. Plumbing systems with septic systems can be overwhelmed by too much use.

New landlords may be surprised to hear of experiences of small apartments being used by multiple families, but it is not that unusual an occurrence. To some the inconvenience is offset by the savings.

Keep in mind the federal law that forbids discrimination against children. Option 1 would be useful, for example, to allow two adults and two children. But if you wanted only two persons in the unit, do not say "2 adults and 0 children," use Option 2 and say "2 persons."

NOTE: *If you are renting a two bedroom apartment and you say that only two persons may rent it, you may be charged with discrimination against children. Be careful.*

TENANT'S
POSITION

Tenants who are considering having children should keep the above note in mind when reviewing such a clause. Federal law may make it impossible to have an eviction for having a child in most cases, but not all. If small studio apartments were limited to two persons and some were rented to single parents with a child, the landlord might be allowed to forbid a couple with a child to rent such a unit.

Certain Number of Adults and Children

OPTION #1

> OCCUPANCY. The premises shall not be occupied by
> more than _____ adults and _____ children.

Any Certain Number of Persons

OPTION #2

OCCUPANCY. The premises shall not be occupied by more than _____ persons.

Fee for Additional Persons

OPTION #3

OCCUPANCY. The premises shall not be occupied by more than _____ adults and _____ children. Tenant shall pay an additional $75 per month for each additional person occupying the premises.

Retroactive Fee for Additional Persons

OPTION #4

OCCUPANCY. The premises shall not be occupied by more than _____ adults and _____ children. Tenant shall pay an additional $75 per month for each additional person occupying the premises. If Tenant fails to inform Landlord of additional occupants, additional rent shall be retroactively due from the beginning of the term of the lease.

Allowance for Guests

OPTION #5

OCCUPANCY. The premises shall not be occupied by more than _____ persons. Such limitation shall not exclude guests who stay two weeks or less.

TENANT'S APPLIANCES

PURPOSE — This clause governs the use of appliances.

LANDLORD'S POSITION — The electrical system in some buildings is not capable of supplying current for large appliances and use of such may cause a fire. Also, where landlords include the electricity in the rent they do not want the tenant to use excessive amounts.

TENANT'S POSITION — The tenant does not want to cause a fire, but does want to use reasonable appliances. If the tenant plans to use an appliance such as a clothes dryer the electrical system of the property should be checked prior to signing the lease and an agreement made with the landlord.

Simple Clause

OPTION #1

TENANT'S APPLIANCES. Tenant agrees not to use any heaters, fixtures, or appliances which draw excessive current, without the written consent of the Landlord.

Clause Allowing Raise in Rent

OPTION #2

TENANT'S APPLIANCES. Tenant agrees not to use any heaters, fixtures, or appliances which draw excessive current, without the written consent of the Landlord. In the event Tenant's appliances cause more electricity to be used than the monthly average for the past year, Tenant shall reimburse Landlord for any excess use.

Permission for Certain Appliances

OPTION #3

TENANT'S APPLIANCES. Tenant agrees not to use any heaters, fixtures or appliances which draw excessive current without the written consent of Landlord. Landlord consents to Tenant's use of a _____ on the premises.

PARKING

PURPOSE | This clause designates parking areas and can also include reference to other vehicles such as boats or trailers.

LANDLORD'S POSITION | The landlord does not want the tenant to park a vehicle on the lawn or to store vehicles on the premises. It is after a tenant decides that his new car is safer in the middle of the front lawn than on the street that the landlord realizes that this is an important clause to include in a lease.

TENANT'S POSITION | In some larger cities there may be virtually no street parking at certain times. Tenants should investigate this before entering into a lease, especially if there is a possibility of having a parking space included in the lease.

Parking in Certain Areas

OPTION #1

> PARKING. Tenant agrees that no parking is allowed on the premises except _____.

Parking in Certain Areas, but No Storage

OPTION #2

> PARKING. Tenant agrees that no parking is allowed on the premises except _____.
> Campers, trailers, boats, recreational vehicles or inoperable vehicles shall not be stored on the premises without written consent of the Landlord.

NOTE: *Sometimes merely prohibiting something is not as successful as imposing a penalty for violation.*

Penalty Storage Fee

OPTION #3

> PARKING. Tenant agrees that no parking is allowed on the premises except _____.Campers, trailers, boats, recreational vehicles or inoperable vehicles shall not be stored on the premises without written consent of the Landlord. Storage without Landlord's permission shall be subject to a $30 per day storage fee.

LIENS

PURPOSE

The landlord wants to be sure that the tenant does not do anything that will cause a *lien* to attach to the landlord's property. For example, if a tenant contracted for some repair to the property, a mechanic's lien or construction lien might be placed by a contractor who was not paid.

LIENS. The estate of the Landlord shall not be subject to any liens for improvements contracted by Tenant.

NOTE: *This clause may not be enforceable in all states. You should check local law. In any case it cannot hurt to use it because even if it is not legally enforceable, it might convince someone who does not know the law.*

WATER BEDS

PURPOSE

This clause determines whether a landlord's consent extra insurance is required for water bed use.

LANDLORD'S
POSITION

The landlord does not want his property damaged by negligent use of a water bed. Due to the success of water bed industry lobbyists it is illegal to forbid such beds in most areas. Most buildings have no trouble holding the weight of a water bed (and would violate building codes if unable to bear the weight), but the biggest risk is from water damage in the event of a leak. Therefore landlords in most areas can require tenants with water beds to carry insurance against liability. This is especially important in an upper floor unit where water can damage property in units below.

The amount of insurance to require depends upon the risk. In some buildings the most that could be damaged would be the floor covering, but in others, such as tall apartment buildings, a leak could result in damage to numerous apartments.

The trouble and expense of getting insurance may deter tenants from renting where insurance is required. Also, some landlords feel that a clause in a lease forbidding water beds may serve as a deterrent to tenants who do not know the law.

TENANT'S
POSITION

If the tenant plans to use a water bed he should be sure that either the lease or state law allows it. (A lease clause forbidding it may be void if state law overrules it.) because of the risk of damage to the building and other tenant's property a tenant with a waterbed should have insurance.

No Permission Required

OPTION #1

WATER BEDS. In the event Tenant uses a flotation type bedding device on the premises, Tenant shall maintain a policy of insurance of at least $_____ to cover any damages from such device and shall list Landlord as a named insured on said policy.

Landlord's Written Permission Required

OPTION #2

WATER BEDS. Tenant shall not use any flotation type bedding device on the premises without Landlord's written consent and insurance covering Landlord for at least $_____ against any damage which might result therefrom.

HOLDOVER BY TENANT

PURPOSE

This clause governs the situation where a tenant stays beyond the lease term.

LANDLORD'S
POSITION

The landlord wants to be sure the tenant vacates the premises on time, and to be sure the terms of the lease still apply if the tenant does not. In many areas these matters are covered by law, but it is always best to spell them out clearly in the lease. Double rent is common because a *holdover tenant* (one who does not leave on time) may cause the landlord other problems if the property has already been rented or sold.

TENANT'S
POSITION

The tenant would prefer to avoid double rent. (Option 3).

Double Monthly Rent

OPTION #1

HOLDOVER BY TENANT. If Tenant fails to deliver possession of the premises to Landlord at the expiration of this lease, the tenancy shall still be governed by this lease on a month-to-month basis. If such holdover is without the consent of the Landlord, Tenant shall be liable for double the monthly rent for each month or fraction thereof.

Double Daily Rent

OPTION #2

HOLDOVER BY TENANT. If Tenant fails to deliver possession of the premises to Landlord at the expiration of this lease, the tenancy shall still be governed by this lease on a month-to-month basis. If such holdover is without the consent of the Landlord, Tenant shall be liable for double the amount of rent due for each day the Tenant holds over. Said daily rent shall be calculated by using one-fifteenth of the last month's rent.

Regular Monthly Rent

OPTION #3

HOLDOVER BY TENANT. If Tenant fails to deliver possession of the premises to Landlord at the expiration of this lease, the tenancy shall still be governed by this lease on a month-to-month basis.

DAMAGE TO PREMISES

PURPOSE

This clause defines the rights of the parties in the event of destruction of the premises.

LANDLORD'S
POSITION

Sometimes the landlord may want to terminate the lease if repairs or expenses become too costly. State law may control the rights of the parties in such situation.

TENANT'S
POSITION

If the premises are damaged or destroyed, the tenant might not want to live there, especially if he has to find temporary quarters elsewhere for several weeks or months. Therefore the tenant would also like the option to terminate the lease.

Landlord May Terminate

OPTION #1

DAMAGE TO PREMISES. In the event the premises are damaged or destroyed by fire or other casualty or are declared uninhabitable by a governmental authority, Landlord may terminate this lease or may repair the premises.

Partial Damage—Tenancy Continues—Landlord Not Liable

OPTION #2

DAMAGE TO PREMISES. In the event the premises are made uninhabitable by fire or other casualty or are declared uninhabitable by a governmental authority, Landlord may terminate this lease or restore the premises to their original condition. In the event the premises are only partially damaged this lease shall continue in full force and effect and the damages shall be repaired at the expense of Landlord. Landlord shall not be liable to Tenant for any inconvenience or annoyance cause by such damage or repairs.

Either Party May Terminate

OPTION #3

DAMAGE TO PREMISES. In the event the premises are damaged or destroyed by fire or other casualty or are declared uninhabitable by a governmental authority, Landlord or Tenant may terminate this lease.

FURNISHINGS

PURPOSE

If any furniture or other specific items are part of the rent property, this clause governs them.

LANDLORD'S
POSITION

If the property is furnished, the landlord will want to keep track of items of furnishings and to be sure they are returned in good condition.

TENANT'S
POSITION

It is also in the tenant's best interest to check the items at the beginning and end of the tenancy to be sure that he or she is not charged for some item that was removed or damaged before he or she arrived at the premises.

FURNISHINGS. Tenant acknowledges receipt of the items listed on "Schedule A" attached hereto and agrees to return them in good condition at the end of this lease.

NOTE: *A SCHEDULE A to list items on is included with the forms in this book. (see form 10, p.189.)*

Pest Control

PURPOSE

Who is responsible for pest control, extermination, etc. is set out in this clause.

LANDLORD'S
POSITION

In most cases the landlord wants the tenant to be responsible for extermination services. In large apartment buildings laws may require that the landlord keep the premises free of pests, but in single family homes and small apartment buildings the landlord may be allowed to transfer that responsibility to the tenant. The logic for the difference is that in a single family home the tenant has complete control over the premises and should be able to keep it free of pests, but in an apartment building the tenant has no control over the neighbors whose lifestyle may encourage such pests.

It is usually not a good idea to make a tenant responsible for treatment for pests like termites because a tenant who can move out in a few months will not care if the landlord's property is being slowly eaten away. The best a landlord can hope for is to be told about evidence of termites and to not be required to put up the tenant in a motel during treatment.

Some areas may require a landlord to put up tenants in a motel during treatment but others only require that the rent be *abated* (suspended) during those days.

TENANT'S
POSITION

In a single family home it is reasonable for the tenant to be responsible for pest treatment unless the property is already infested. In a building with more than one unit, a tenant may have a hopeless task of fighting off pests if the neighbors' units are infested. If a tenant is asked to vacate the premises while the property is treated, he should check state law to see if the landlord is required to pay for temporary accommodations.

Tenant Notifies for Termites—
Tenant Responsible for Living Arrangements

OPTION #1

PEST CONTROL. Tenant agrees to be responsible for pest control and extermination services on the premises, and to keep the premises clean and sanitary to avoid such problems. Tenant shall notify Landlord immediately of any evidence of termites. Landlord shall not be responsible to provide living arrangements for Tenant in the event the premises must be vacated for termite or other pest control treatment.

Tenant's Responsibility

OPTION #2

PEST CONTROL. Tenant agrees to be responsible for pest control and extermination services on the premises, and to keep the premises clean and sanitary to avoid such problems.

Landlord's Responsibility

OPTION #3

PEST CONTROL. Tenant shall keep the premises in a clean and sanitary condition and shall notify Landlord in the event of infestation. Landlord shall arrange for treatment.

COMMERCIAL LEASE CLAUSES 9

This chapter contains various provisions applicable to commercial leases. You should also review the provisions in Chapters 8 and 10 to see if any of them can be adapted to your commercial lease situation.

As in Chapter 7 (see page 37) there are various options for the clauses in these leases.

PREMISES

PURPOSE   The lease must accurately describe the areas leased to the tenant.

LANDLORD'S POSITION   To avoid any problems, a landlord should charge a fixed rental rate for a unit and list the size as approximate.

TENANT'S POSITION   The rental rate in many commercial leases is based upon a fixed rate per square foot of rented space. Sometimes the figure used by the landlord is incorrect and the tenant pays higher rent than required. Tenants have occasionally confronted the landlord with the error and demanded a rebate of the overcharge. (Six inches along a fifty foot wall is twenty-five square feet and at $10 a square foot this would be $250. There are companies which will accurately measure a tenant's unit on the condition that they will get a percentage of any money saved in lower rent.

Simple Clause

OPTION #1

PREMISES. The premises leased by Tenant consist of a
_____ of approximately _____
square feet located at _____
together with the common use with other Tenants of all
parking, roads and walkways and other public areas.

Inclusion of Utility Systems

OPTION #2

PREMISES. The premises leased by Tenant consist of a
_____ of approximately _____
square feet located at _____
including all plumbing, electrical, sewerage, heating, air
conditioning and other utilities fixtures, lines, equipment,
pipes, cables and posts thereof together with the common
use with other Tenants of all parking, roads and walkways
and other public areas.

Measured from Outside Walls

OPTION #3

PREMISES. The premises leased by Tenant consist of a

_____ of approximately

_____ square feet located at

_____ as measured

from exterior surfaces of outside walls and center lines of

dividing walls including all plumbing, electrical, sewerage,

heating, air conditioning and other utilities fixtures, lines,

equipment, pipes, cables and posts thereof together with

the common use with other Tenants of all parking, roads

and walkways and other public areas.

TERM

PURPOSE The period of occupancy should be clear.

LANDLORD'S POSITION The landlord usually likes to have long term tenants, but it is also important to the landlord that the rent keep up with taxes, expenses, and other costs. The landlord could lose a lot of money, especially if he has an *adjustable rate loan* (the interest rate on the landlord's mortgage changes with the market interest rates).

TENANT'S POSITION When leasing commercial property in a good location, the tenant would usually prefer to obtain a lease for the longest term possible. This is especially true where the tenant has spent considerable sums remodeling the premises, such as for a restaurant. If the tenant plans to sell the business it will usually be more valuable with a long-term lease. Two reasons the tenant might not want a long-term lease are if the location is questionable or if the business is new. If the business fails the tenant might be stuck with payments on a five or ten year lease.

A tenant would ideally like to be able to get out of a lease early if he is unable to continue the business as a result of illness or bankruptcy, however, it is not easy to get a landlord to agree to such an escape clause. A tenant whose business is successful would like the ability to renew the lease at favorable terms. This is handled by the "Renewal" clause on page 105.

OPTION #1

TERM. The term of this lease shall be for a period of _____ months commencing at 12:01 a.m. on _____, _____ and ending at midnight on _____, _____.

OPTION #2

TERM. The term of this lease shall be for a period of ___ months commencing at 12:01 a.m. on _____, ___ and ending at midnight on _____, ____. In the event of the permanent closure of Tenant's business this lease shall terminate.

Rent

PURPOSE

The amount of rent should be clear. If sales or use tax is charged on commercial rent then the lease should spell out which party must pay it. Different courts (even in the same state) have ruled both for the tenant and the landlord where the lease was not clear.

LANDLORD'S POSITION

For a long-term lease, the landlord would want an escalation clause to cover increased costs and inflation. Consider the effect of inflation if it returned to 13%. After five years, a monthly rent of $1000 would be worth only $540. If the landlord has an adjustable rate loan on the property it is imperative that the rent also be adjustable.

Some landlords raise the rent a fixed amount each year. Others tie rent increases to increases in taxes or the *Consumer Price Index (CPI)* (the government's measure of inflation). Usually landlords provide for increases in rent but not for decreases in case of deflation or depression.

One way for a landlord to be sure to cover costs is to charge a fixed rent plus a percentage of the other costs of the property such as taxes and maintenance. Because of the ease of *padding* costs (adding costs under the guise of something else, like utilities) the tenant should be sure to include in the lease an exact description of what costs will be charged and how they will be computed.

In some commercial rentals the landlord charges a percentage of the tenant's gross sales in addition to a fixed amount of base rent. This allows the tenant to pay less during slow periods and more when business is good. One variation of this is to charge a percentage only on sales over a certain amount. The landlord must keep in mind, however, that it is not always easy to be sure what a tenant's business is taking in.

TENANT'S POSITION

With the current state of our economy there is also the possibility of deflation. With deflation, rent that normally stayed the same would be going up each year for the tenant. To protect against deflation the tenant would prefer the rent indexed to the CPI rather than raised a fixed amount each year.

Simple Rent Clause
(use with "Rent Adjustment" clause on page 104)

OPTION #1

RENT. The rent for the term of this lease shall be $_____ per month, together with any sales or use tax due for the rental of the premises.

Simple Rent Clause with Percentage Escalation

OPTION #2

RENT. The rent for the first year of this lease shall be $_____ per month, together with any sales or use tax due for the rental of the premises. For the second and each subsequent year under this lease the rent shall be increased by the same percentage of increase as the "Consumer Price Index - All Items - U. S. City Average" for the previous twelve months.

Rent Clauses with Additional Payments for Taxes, Utilities, and Maintenance

OPTION #3

RENT. The base rent for the term of this lease shall be $_____ per month plus _____% of the charges for real estate taxes, utilities and maintenance of the common areas, together with any sales or use tax due for the rental of the premises.

Additional Payments plus Percentage Escalation

OPTION #4

RENT. The base rent for the first year of this lease shall be $_____ per month. For the second and each subsequent year under this lease the rent shall be increased by the same percentage of increase as the of the "Consumer Price Index - All Items - U. S. City Average" for the previous twelve months. In addition to the base rent the Tenant shall pay _____% of the charges for real estate taxes, utilities and maintenance of the common areas, together with any sales or use tax due for the rental of the premises.

Additional Payment Based on All Sales

OPTION #5

RENT. The base rent for the term of this lease shall be $_____ per month plus _____% of the gross receipts from the premises, together with any sales or use tax due for the rental of the premises.

Additional Payment Based on Excess Sales

OPTION #6

RENT. The base rent for the term of this lease shall be $_____ per month plus _____% of the gross receipts from the premises which exceed $_____ per month, together with any sales or use tax due for the rental of the premises.

NOTE: *When using Option 5 or 6, you should also use Clause 3 on page 137.*

RENT ADJUSTMENTS

PURPOSE

Adjustments allow for raises in rent for inflation. Some parties prefer to break up the payment clause into separate clauses to make negotiation easier. When using the simple rent clause these clauses can be added.

LANDLORD'S POSITION

The landlord would prefer Option 1 in which the rent can only rise. His second choice would be Option 2 in which it can decrease, but not lower than the initial rent.

TENANT'S POSITION

The tenant would prefer that the rent is fixed during the entire lease so he would not want any of these clauses. But of all of them, he would prefer Option 3 in which it can either increase or decrease with inflation. Next he would prefer Option 2.

OPTION #1

RENT ADJUSTMENTS. The base rent shall be raised at the first month of each year in the same percentage as any rise in the "Consumer Price Index - All Items - U. S. City Average."

Option 1 calls for the rent to rise with inflation but not to be lowered with deflation.

OPTION #2

RENT ADJUSTMENTS. The base rent shall be adjusted at the first month of each year in the same percentage as the "Consumer Price Index - All Items - U. S. City Average" has changed in the prior year, provided however, that the minimum rent shall not be less than the initial rent under this lease.

Option 2 allows the rent to fluctuate according to the inflation or deflation rate with a minimum of the first year's rate.

OPTION #3

RENT ADJUSTMENTS. The base rent shall be adjusted at the first month of each year in the same percentage as the "Consumer Price Index - All Items - U. S. City Average" has changed in the prior year.

Option 3 allows the rent to fluctuate with inflation or deflation.

RENEWAL

PURPOSE

Renewal allows for an extension of the lease at predetermined terms. The parties should consider the possibility of inflation or deflation here as well. After ten years of 13% inflation $1000 rent would be worth only $290. This would be great for the tenant, but it would lower the value of the building to the landlord. If the initial lease contains fixed increases, then the renewal would usually include fixed increases. If the initial lease included increases based upon the inflation rate then the renewal usually includes fixed increases.

LANDLORD'S
POSITION

The landlord would like to get the most rent possible without putting the tenant out of business or driving him away. During periods of high inflation it is usually better to base the increase on the inflation rate. During times without inflation or with deflation, a fixed increase in the lease usually provides more rent. However, if inflation rises while a fixed increase lease is in effect, the landlord could end up undercharging for rent.

TENANT'S
POSITION

The tenant wants the increases, if any, to be as low as possible. During times of inflation a small fixed increase would usually be best, but during non-inflationary or deflationary times, an increase based upon the inflation rate would be best.

Rent Increase Based on CPI

OPTION #1

RENEWAL. Providing that Tenant is not in default under any term of this lease, Tenant is hereby given an option to renew this lease for a term of _____ years. The base rent for the first year of the renewal shall be the amount of rent for the previous year plus the percentage increase of the of the "Consumer Price Index - All Items - U. S. City Average." (CPI) for the previous twelve months. For each subsequent year the rent shall increase* according to the CPI. Tenant shall give Landlord written notice sixty (60) days prior to the end of this lease of intent to renew.

* The tenant would prefer the phrase "increase or decrease" in the clause.

Rent Increase Based on Prior Increases

OPTION #2

> RENEWAL. Providing that Tenant is not in default under any term of this lease, Tenant is hereby given an option to renew this lease for a term of _____ years. The rent for the renewal term shall be calculated according to the same rate of increase as used during the original term of this lease. Tenant shall give Landlord written notice sixty (60) days prior to the end of this lease of his intent to renew.

TAXES

PURPOSE   If the payment clause did not cover the payment of taxes, an additional clause should be added to clarify each party's responsibility. The important thing is to be clear about exactly who pays the taxes.

LANDLORD'S
POSITION   The landlord wants to be sure that any increases in taxes are paid by the tenants so any of these clauses would work depending on the number of tenants and whether taxes are included in the rent.

TENANT'S
POSITION   The tenant would prefer fixed rent with no additional payment for taxes so he would prefer to omit this clause.

Tenant Pays All Applicable Taxes
plus a Share of Real Estate Taxes

OPTION #1

> TAXES. Tenant shall pay to Landlord along with the rent, any sales or use tax payable to any governmental authority. Tenant shall also pay the real estate taxes attributable to the premises. Tenants amount of taxes shall be _____% of Landlord's tax bill covering these premises. Real estate taxes shall be paid monthly along with rent and shall be based upon one-twelfth of the most recent annual bill.

Option 1 is for a situation where several tenants each pay a percentage of the tax bill.

Tenant Pays All Applicable plus
Only Increases of Real Estate Taxes

OPTION #2

> TAXES. Tenant shall pay to Landlord along with the rent, any sales or use tax payable to any governmental authority. In the event the real estate taxes attributable to the premises are raised for any future year under this agreement, Tenant shall pay each month an amount of such increase proportional to Tenant's portion of the premises in addition to the rent payment.

Option 2 is for a situation where the taxes are included in the rent, but the tenant is expected to pay any increases. Depending on the agreement between the parties it is possible to combine these to create other options such as where several tenants split the increase in taxes.

USE OF PREMISES

PURPOSE

To insure that the tenant does not use the premises for any illegal or dangerous purpose or compete with other tenants, include this clause.

LANDLORD'S
POSITION

The landlord does not want any dangerous activity on the premises. In some cases a landlord wants to limit the type of business a tenant operates because he has agreed to let another tenant have the exclusive right to that type of business.

In a building that does not have other tenants the landlord is not as concerned about the type of business. However, landlords should keep in mind that some tenants, such as professionals make a property more valuable than other tenants, such as fireworks manufacturers.

TENANT'S
POSITION

A clause that limits the use of the premises to one business is not good for the tenant. The tenant might decide to expand the business or to add more profitable products and does not want to be limited to the original purpose. Ideally the tenant would like to be able to do anything that is not illegal, but if that is not acceptable to the landlord, then try to include as long a list as possible of permissible uses.

Simple Clause

OPTION #1

USE. The premises shall not be used for any illegal purpose or in violation of any zoning laws or property restrictions.

Specified Use

OPTION #2

USE. The premises shall be used only as _____ and shall not be used for any illegal purpose or in violation of any zoning laws or property restrictions.

Specified Use Plus Displays Restrictions

OPTION #3

USE. The premises shall be used only as _____ and shall not be used for any illegal purpose or in violation of any zoning laws or property restrictions. Tenant shall not keep or display any merchandise in any common areas without the written consent of the Landlord. Tenant shall maintain any display windows in neat and clear condition and shall not make any structural alterations to the premises without the written consent of the Landlord.

Specified Use plus Multiple Restrictions

OPTION #4

USE. The premises shall be used only as _____ and shall not be used for any illegal purpose or in violation of any zoning laws or property restrictions. Tenant shall not keep or display any merchandise in any common areas without the written consent of the Landlord. Tenant shall maintain any display windows in neat and clear condition and shall not make any structural alterations to the premises without the written consent of the Landlord. Tenant agrees to at all times conduct his business in a reputable manner and to not hold any auctions, liquidations, fire, or bankruptcy sale without the written consent of the Landlord, which consent shall not reasonably be withheld.

ENVIRONMENTAL LAWS

PURPOSE

The environmental laws are so strict today that property owners can face devastating fines or loss of their property for violations. This clause ensures compliance with the laws and provides for remedies if the laws are not followed.

> ENVIRONMENTAL LAWS. Tenant shall strictly comply with any and all local, state and federal environmental laws and regulations. In the event Tenant violates any such laws the Landlord may terminate this lease. Tenant shall remain liable for the cleanup of any such violation and for any other costs, fines or penalties based upon such violation.

Landlords can be held personally liable for environmental cleanup even if it is greater than the value of the property. This means your $100,000 investment in a gas station property could cost you $500,000 in damages if the gas tanks leak into the ground.

Landlords can even be held liable for property that was polluted before they bought it or which is not discovered to be polluted until after they sell it. Because of this it is important to have property checked before it is purchased. Property records can show what previous owners might have had polluting businesses and tests can determine if the property is currently polluted. Unfortunately these tests are expensive.

COMPETING BUSINESSES

PURPOSE

This clause lays out the guidelines for renting to other businesses competing with the tenant. The parties should decide exactly what they are agreeing to and spell it out clearly in the lease. If a lease says that the landlord will not allow another pet store in the shopping center, can the landlord rent to a large department store that will sell pet supplies at a discount? Probably yes (depending upon the judge) if the store is just a general department store and not a pet store.

LANDLORD'S POSITION

Ideally a landlord would not want to limit who he can rent other units to, but some tenants refuse to rent unless they are assured that there will not be an identical business a few doors away. A landlord can agree to these clauses if he is sure that he won't have a much better opportunity with a future tenant. For example, if he rents to a quick stop food mart and agrees not to allow other tenants to sell food, he will be unable to rent to a major supermarket chain.

TENANT'S POSITION

The tenant does not want other businesses in the same shopping center to compete with him for customers. In large shopping centers it is common for a tenant to want the exclusive right to sell certain products. If too many tenants are selling the same thing, some or all of them may go out of business.

If the tenant does not want anyone else selling pet supplies in the shopping center he should ask for that in the lease. But the landlord must realize that he might possibly lose a big tenant.

The tenant should check local zoning laws and regulations prior to signing the lease to be sure that the intended business may be legally carried out on the premises. Once the lease is signed it may be too late.

Basic Clause

OPTION #1

> COMPETING BUSINESSES. Landlord agrees not to rent other units in the building to _____ businesses during the term of this lease and any extensions of this lease.

Additional Limitation on Certain Items

OPTION #2

> COMPETING BUSINESSES. Landlord agrees not to rent other units in the building to _____ businesses during the term of this lease and any extensions of this lease. In addition, Landlord shall prohibit other businesses in the building from offering for sale _____.

PARKING AREAS

PURPOSE

The lease should clearly designate which areas a tenant may or may not use for parking. (Because parking regulations can be lengthy, it is better if they are not included in the lease. This also allows them to be amended from time to time to accommodate changed circumstances.)

LANDLORD'S POSITION

The landlord wants to be sure that parking is adequate for all tenants. One good rule to have is to limit employee parking to remote areas of the lot. For each employee who takes a front spot in the morning, a hundred customers may have to walk across the lot. Employees only go to and from their cars once and should not be allowed to take the most convenient spots.

TENANT'S POSITION

Tenants should check that parking is adequate before leasing the premises. Find out what kind of businesses share the lot and ask other tenants if there is adequate parking. For example, a government office such as social security or food stamps could completely fill the parking lot frequently. Tenant should beware of parking rules that can change because they could become unworkable.

Limited Areas

OPTION #1

PARKING AREAS. Tenant shall have the nonexclusive use of parking space for _____ cars. The use of such parking areas shall at all times be subject to such reasonable rules and regulations as Landlord shall promulgate.

Unlimited Areas

OPTION #2

PARKING AREAS. Tenant shall have the nonexclusive use of all parking areas about the premises. Parking areas are intended primarily for use by customers and Tenant shall not permit its employees to use such areas for the parking or storage of any automobiles, trucks or other vehicles except as may be approved and designated in writing by Landlord. The use of such parking areas shall at all times be subject to such reasonable rules and regulations as Landlord shall promulgate.

SIGNS AND ADVERTISING

PURPOSE

This clause governs how signs can be posted.

LANDLORD'S
POSITION

The landlord wants to be able to approve signs placed on the property. Use of the name or picture of the property in the wrong context may also cause problems for the landlord. To insure that unreasonable signs or devices are not used by the tenant and that the name of the premises is not used without permission, include a clause on signs and advertising. Unusual signs may be too gaudy, dangerous, or even illegal.

TENANT'S
POSITION

The tenant will usually want to have as visible a sign as possible to attract business. This should be negotiated before signing the lease. If the tenant is not allowed to have an adequate sign the business may suffer. For the best protection the tenant should have a clear description of the type and location of sign agreed upon. This can be described in an attached exhibit to the lease.

On some properties the landlord will have one uniform type of signage used for all tenants. This may be over each unit or on one structure near the street. Usually the landlord has contracted with one sign company to create uniform signs. The tenant should confirm that the price is reasonable and does not include any kickback or other hidden cost.

Extensive Conditions

OPTION #1

SIGNS & ADVERTISING. Tenant shall have the right to install and maintain at his own expense, a storefront sign subject to the written approval of the Landlord as to dimensions, location and design, which approval shall not be unreasonably withheld. Tenant agrees not to use any advertising media in the premises or common areas that shall be deemed objectionable to the Landlord or other Tenants such as loudspeakers, radio broadcasts or recorded music which can be heard outside the leased premises. Tenant shall not install any exterior awnings, banners or lighting without the written consent of the Landlord. Tenant shall not use the name of the premises except as the address, or use any picture or likeness of the premises without the written consent of the Landlord.

Sign Rules

OPTION #2

SIGNS & ADVERTISING. Tenant shall not erect any signs or other devices outside the premises without the prior written consent of the Landlord.

Only Specific Signs

OPTION #3

SIGNS & ADVERTISING. Tenant shall be allowed to place a sign on the property as described in Exhibit ___ attached to this lease.

Maintenance and Repair

PURPOSE
Which party is responsible for each type of maintenance to the premises should be designated. (The more detailed this clause the less likely a disagreement will arise.)

LANDLORD'S POSITION
The landlord would like to be responsible for as little maintenance as possible, but in buildings with more than one tenant he usually retains the responsibility for the exterior. Sometimes this is reimbursed by the tenants.

TENANT'S POSITION
The tenant would like to be responsible for as little maintenance as possible but is usually responsible for systems within his unit. In a single-tenant building the tenant may be responsible for all maintenance. In multi-unit building tenant may be required to pay a portion of the exterior maintenance.

If the tenant pays a percentage of the common maintenance these costs should be explained clearly in writing in advance. Find out if maintenance is handled by a company that the landlord controls or has connections with and check with other tenants and see what the maintenance charges have been in the past year or two. (This clause reduces the risk of *padding*, or hidden costs, when written as detailed as possible.)

The following are two options. Depending upon your arrangement you may wish to shift around duties.

Tenant Responsible for Repairs

OPTION #1

MAINTENANCE & REPAIR. The Landlord shall keep the foundation, outer walls and roof of the premises and the common areas in good repair, except that Landlord shall not be liable for any repairs occasioned by the acts of Tenant, its agents or employees. Tenant shall be responsible for maintenance and repair to the inside of the premises including heating and cooling systems, electrical, plumbing, machinery, hardware, doors, windows, screens and painting. All such repairs shall be made with materials and workmanship equivalent to the original. Tenant shall be responsible for extermination service to the premises.

Tenant Pays a Percentage of Repairs

OPTION #2

MAINTENANCE & REPAIR. The Landlord shall keep the foundation, outer walls and roof of the premises and the common areas in good repair, except that Landlord shall not be liable for any repairs occasioned by the acts of Tenant, its agents or employees. Tenant shall be responsible for reimbursing Landlord monthly for ___% of any amounts expended by Landlord for maintenance and repair. Tenant shall be responsible for maintenance and repair to the inside of the premises including heating and cooling systems, electrical, plumbing, machinery, hardware, doors, windows, screens and painting. All such repairs shall be made with materials and workmanship equivalent to the original. Tenant shall be responsible for extermination service to the premises.

NOTE: *In many cases the tenant pays all maintenance. In other situations part is handled directly by the tenant, and building maintenance is handled by the landlord but paid proportionally by each tenant.*

UTILITIES

PURPOSE

It should be clear which party is responsible for paying utilities. The setup of the building may dictate who pays for each charge.

LANDLORD'S POSITION

The landlord usually wants all utility costs passed through to the tenants. If they cannot be billed directly to the tenants, the reimbursement procedure should be clearly spelled out.

TENANT'S POSITION

If the landlord provides heat and air conditioning, the tenant should be sure that they are provided during all hours that the tenant plans to use the premises. Some landlords turn off these services on weekends and holidays. If the tenant plans for his business to be open those days, this should be negotiated before executing the lease, and listed as a separate exhibit.

If the tenant is to reimburse the landlord for some utilities the method determining the amount should be determined prior to execution of the lease. Some landlords may pad these bills, for example by charging a flat fee for electricity that is well above the amount paid to the utility company. This may be illegal in some states, since the landlord is probably not licensed as a utility company. It may be forbidden either by statute or by rule of the commission that regulates utilities.

Tenant Pays All

OPTION #1

UTILITIES. The Tenant shall be responsible for all charges for electricity, gas, water, sewer or other utilities supplied to the premises. Any such charges not billed directly to Tenant shall be reimbursed to Landlord each month upon presentation of a statement.

Tenant Pays Percentage

OPTION #2

UTILITIES. The Tenant shall be responsible for all charges for electricity, gas, water, sewer or other utilities supplied to the premises. Tenant shall pay _____% of the bills for _____ within 10 days of receipt from Landlord.

Each Party Pays Part

OPTION #3

UTILITIES. The Tenant shall be responsible for _____ and the Landlord shall be responsible for _____.

Landlord Pays

OPTION #4

UTILITIES. The Landlord shall provide to Tenant during usual business hours, heat and air conditioning, water and sewer, window washing, janitorial services and electricity for routine lighting and routine 110 volt appliances. If Tenant's use exceeds reasonable amounts as compared to other Tenants, then Landlord may require Tenant to pay the excess.

Landlord Pays—Days and Times Limited

OPTION #5

UTILITIES. The Landlord shall provide to Tenant heat and air conditioning, water and sewer, window washing, janitorial services and electricity for routine lighting and routine 110 volt appliances. These services shall be provided during the days and times listed on exhibit ___.

LIABILITY

PURPOSE

This clause outlines the extent to which each party is responsible for things like damages, loss, injury, or theft.

LANDLORD'S
POSITION

The landlord will want protection from liability for injury or damage on the leased premises. In most cases a landlord cannot limit his liability for his own negligence with a clause in the lease. Occasionally a landlord may be sued for some act of a tenant. While insurance usually covers this situation, the landlord may also want to require the tenant to be liable for any such expenses.

TENANT'S
POSITION

The tenant does not want to be liable for any acts of the landlord and does not want to defend the landlord in any suit. However, this may be covered by an insurance policy on the tenant's business. (See the next section on insurance.)

Extensive Clause Protecting Landlord

OPTION #1

LIABILITY. Landlord, its employees and agents shall not be liable for and Tenant will indemnify and save them harmless from, all fines, suits, claims, demands, losses and actions (including attorney's fees) for any injury to person or damage to, or loss of property on or about the premises, caused by the negligence or misconduct or breach of this lease by Tenant, its employees, subtenants, invitees, or by any other person entering the premises. Landlord shall not be liable for any loss or damages to any person or property occasioned by theft, fire, act of God, public emergency, injunction, riot, strike, war, insurrection, court order, requisitions of other governmental body or authority, by other Tenants of the building, their invitees, or by any other matter beyond control of Landlord, or from any cause whatever except Landlord's negligence. Tenant hereby acknowledges that Landlord has made no written or oral representations or warranties, either express or implied, as to any security measures or safeguards on or about the premises.

Tenant Holds Landlord Harmless

OPTION #2

LIABILITY. Tenant agrees to hold Landlord harmless from any and all claims for injuries or damages occurring on the premises, and to be solely responsible for insuring Tenant's own possessions on the premises.

Agree That Landlord Is Not Liable

OPTION #3

LIABILITY. It is expressly agreed between the parties that Landlord shall not be liable for any injury or for damage to property on or about the leased premises.

Landlord Liable Only for His or Her Own Act

OPTION #4

LIABILITY. Landlord shall not be liable for any loss or injury on the premises not caused by Landlord. Tenant agrees to be responsible for insurance of Tenant's own property if desired.

Landlord Holds Tenant Harmless

OPTION #5

LIABILITY. Landlord shall not be liable for any loss or injury on the premises not caused by Landlord. Tenant agrees to be responsible for insurance of Tenant's own property if desired. Landlord shall hold tenant harmless from any injuries arising on the common areas about the property.

Option 5 protects the tenant from liability for injuries that happen in the common areas that the tenant has no responsibility to maintain.

INSURANCE

PURPOSE
This clause outlines the types of insurance required.

LANDLORD'S POSITION
The landlord wants to be sure the tenant maintains current liability insurance to protect the landlord from claims arising out of the tenant's operations. The tenant should not object to this as it is even more important to the tenant to have insurance on the business. The landlord should be sure that he is listed on the tenant's policy as a loss payee. The landlord should also have his own policy. Every landlord should consider an umbrella policy of $1,000,000 or more. Today many jury awards approach this amount. It is often possible to get such a policy for a couple hundred dollars a year.

TENANT'S POSITION
The tenant wants to be sure that the landlord has the building insured. To be sure the policy does not expire, the tenant can request to be an additional insured on the policy or to be given notice if it expires. The tenant can also negotiate that the lease can be cancelled if the insurance lapses. The landlord would not be able to reasonably object to this.

Tenant Carries Insurance

OPTION #1

INSURANCE. Tenant shall keep in effect for the term of this lease a policy of liability insurance covering Tenant and Landlord against any liability arising out of any injury on or about the premises. The limit of said policy shall be $_____/$_____ for personal injury and $_____ for property damage. Landlord shall be a loss payee on said policy.

Both Parties Carry Insurance

OPTION #2

INSURANCE. Tenant shall keep in effect for the term of this lease a policy of liability insurance covering Tenant and Landlord against any liability arising out of any injury on or about the premises. The limit of said policy shall be $_____/$_____ for personal injury and $_____ for property damage. Landlord shall keep in effect a policy of casualty insurance on the building and of liability insurance on the common areas.

FIRE OR CASUALTY

PURPOSE

This clause governs what happens in the event of fire or other damage.

LANDLORD'S
POSITION

The landlord wants to be sure the lease will continue and that he will have adequate time to rebuild in the event of fire or other damage to the premises.

TENANT'S
POSITION

The tenant wants the exact opposite. Usually, if the premises are damaged or destroyed the tenant still has to pay the rent until they are restored. This means that the tenant may have to pay rent on both the damaged premises and the temporary premises until restoration is complete. This may be covered by insurance, but additional protection may be added to the lease.

Landlord Repairs Premises—Rent and Insurance Affected

OPTION #1

FIRE OR CASUALTY. In the event of a fire or other casualty to the premises:

a) If the premises are not rendered untenantable in whole or in part, Landlord shall promptly, after receipt of insurance proceeds, repair the premises and the rent shall not abate.

b) If the premises are rendered partially untenantable, Landlord shall promptly, after receipt of insurance proceeds, repair the premises, and the rent shall abate as to the untenantable part of the premises.

c) If the premises are rendered totally untenantable, Landlord shall promptly, after receipt of insurance proceeds, rebuild the premises and the rent shall abate. If such occurs during the last two years of lease, Landlord may cancel this lease.

The rent abatement shall not apply if Tenant has business interruption insurance. In the event that a mortgage holder requires that the insurance proceeds be used to retire the debt then Landlord may cancel this lease.

Basic Clause—Repair within 90 Days

OPTION #2

FIRE OR CASUALTY. In the event the premises are partially damaged by fire or other casualty, Landlord shall repair same within ninety (90) days. In the event the premises are destroyed and untenantable the rent shall abate and Landlord may rebuild the premises within ninety (90) days or may cancel this lease.

Tenant May Cancel

OPTION #3

FIRE OR CASUALTY. In the event the premises are damaged in whole or in part by fire or other casualty, Tenant may cancel this lease. If Tenant elects to continue under the lease the rent shall be abated for the portion of the premises which is unusable.

EMINENT DOMAIN

PURPOSE
: *Eminent domain* is the right of a government body to take part or all of a property for a public use, such as to widen a road or build a public facility.

LANDLORD'S POSITION
: If any part of the property is taken by eminent domain, the landlord will want to receive all the payment attributable to the property. If only part of the property is taken the landlord might want to terminate the lease or continue it at a prorated amount of rent.

TENANT'S POSITION
: The tenant would prefer to have the option of either continuing the business and getting paid for the lowered value, or to terminate the lease and leave if the value of the property is diminished substantially. If the tenant has made substantial improvements to the property he would like to be paid for these out of the award if he is forced to leave.

Landlord Gets Award—Tenancy Continues— Prorated Rent

OPTION #1
: EMINENT DOMAIN. In the event any part of the premises is taken by eminent domain the Landlord shall be entitled to all damages awarded for diminution of the fee and leasehold. In the event that only part of the premises is taken and the remainder is still tenantable, the rent shall be prorated and the Tenant only liable for the portion of the premises still usable.

Landlord Gets Award—Tenancy Terminates

OPTION #2
: EMINENT DOMAIN. In the event any part of the premises is taken by eminent domain the Landlord shall be entitled to all damages awarded for diminution of the fee and leasehold and this lease shall terminate.

Landlord and Tenant Share Award

OPTION #3

> EMINENT DOMAIN. In the event any part of the premises is taken by eminent domain the Landlord shall be entitled to all damages awarded for diminution of the fee and leasehold. If the whole property is taken this lease shall terminate. If part of the property is taken but the premises included in this lease is still tenantable, the Landlord shall have the option to terminate this lease or to continue the lease with the rent prorated and the Tenant only liable for the portion of the premises still usable.

Landlord and Tenant Share Award—Lease Terminates

OPTION #4

> EMINENT DOMAIN. In the event the premises are taken by eminent domain, the Landlord shall be entitled to all damages awarded for diminution of the fee and leasehold and Tenant shall be entitled to all damages awarded for his fixtures and leasehold improvements. In the event the premises are rendered useless by the taking then the Tenant may terminate this lease.

ASSIGNMENT AND SUBLETTING

PURPOSE

This clause explains whether assignment or subleasing are allowed. (see page 75 for a definition of both.)

LANDLORD'S
POSITION

The landlord will want to approve any future tenants of the premises. Although the landlord can usually still go after the original tenant for rent or liability, a new tenant not screened by the landlord might cause problems.

One way around a clause forbidding *assignment* or *subleasing* is if the tenant is a corporation. In such cases, the stock in the corporation can be sold to the new tenant. This way the lease is still in the original name of the corporation and there is no violation of the lease though the ownership of the business has changed. The landlord would prefer to forbid such a maneuver.

TENANT'S
POSITION

The tenant would prefer to keep the right to assign or sublease the premises. In some cases the purpose of starting a business is to sell it in a few years and the location is often a large part of the value. Also, business or health problems could necessitate a sale of the business.

In some states the law requires the landlord to be reasonable about allowing assignments.

No Assignment without Consent

OPTION #1

ASSIGNMENT & SUBLETTING. The Tenant shall not assign this lease or in any manner transfer any interest in the premises or sublet the premises or any part thereof without the written consent of the Landlord.

Corporation Sale Forbidden

OPTION #2

ASSIGNMENT & SUBLETTING. The tenant shall not assign this lease or in any manner transfer any interest in the premises or sublet the premises or any part thereof without the written consent of the Landlord. In the event Tenant is a corporation, and control thereof changes at any time, Landlord may declare such event a default under the lease.

Assignment Allowed if Reasonable

OPTION #3

ASSIGNMENT & SUBLETTING. The Tenant shall not assign this lease or sublet the premises without the written consent of the Landlord. Such consent shall not unreasonably be withheld.

DEFAULT AND REMEDIES

PURPOSE

This clause dictates how to deal with lease violations.

LANDLORD'S
POSITION

If a tenant defaults under any terms of the lease the landlord wants to be able to force the tenant to quickly cure the default or to vacate the premises. Option 2 below contains many extra remedies, but in some states these may be forbidden by law. The landlord would prefer to be able to choose the best one, but in some states the law does not allow a choice of remedies.

This clause is one of the most important in the lease and you should check your state law to see what is legal. One way to do this is to obtain copies of any lease forms promulgated by the bar association or Board of Realtors.®

If a tenant files for bankruptcy the landlord should check with an attorney who specializes in bankruptcy law to learn what options are available. The moment a *bankruptcy* petition is filed all actions against the debtor must stop and a landlord can be held in contempt of court for taking any action against the tenant until permission is given by the court.

TENANT'S
POSITION

The tenant has the opposite interest from the landlord. He wants to have as long as possible to cure the default and he does not want to lose his rights to the property. It is important for the tenant to have written notice of any default and enough time to cure it.

Landlord's Options

OPTION #1

DEFAULT/REMEDIES. In the event the Tenant fails to pay the rent, violates any of the terms of this lease, abandons the premises, transfers any interest in the premises by operation of law, in bankruptcy or by assignment to creditors, then Tenant shall be in default under this lease. Upon such default, Landlord may terminate this lease and retake possession for his own account, or may terminate this lease and retake possession for the account of Tenant, holding Tenant liable for any lost rent, or may let the unit sit vacant and declare the entire remaining balance of the rent immediately due and payable.

Default Defined—Landlord's Options

DEFAULT/REMEDIES. Tenant shall be in default under this lease upon the occurrence of any of the following events:

a)   Failure to pay the rent under this lease;

b)   Failure to perform any other obligation under this lease;

c)   Abandonment of the premises or failure to actively operate the business for which the premises were leased;

d)   The filing by or on behalf of Tenant of any petition or pleading to declare Tenant a bankrupt;

e)   The appointment by any Court of any receiver, trustee or custodian of the property or business of Tenant;

f)   The assignment of any of Tenant's property for the benefit of creditors;

g)   The levy of execution, attachment or other taking of property of Tenant in satisfaction of any judgement, debt or claim.

In the event of any default by Tenant, Landlord may exercise any of the following remedies:

a)   To terminate this lease and retake possession with or without process of law;

b)   To retake possession of the premises for the account of Tenant as Tenant's agent for the remainder of the term or for such shorter period as shall be sufficient in Landlord's judgment to cure the default, thereupon to reinstate the Tenant upon such conditions as the Landlord shall determine to be sufficient to preclude further default;

c)   Without terminating this lease, to demand immediate payment of the entire unpaid balance of the rent;

d)   To retake the premises and to bring an action for damages caused by Tenant's default;

e)   To exercise all of the foregoing remedies cumulatively with each other and with all other rights and remedies which Landlord may have in law or in equity.

Certified Notice to Tenant—Termination Allowed

OPTION #3

DEFAULT/REMEDIES. In the event Tenant fails to pay the rent, violates any of the terms of this lease or abandons the premises, then Tenant shall be given 10 days notice by certified mail to cure such default. If Tenant fails to cure such violation, Tenant shall be in default under this lease and Landlord shall be entitled to terminate this lease.

Certified Notice to Tenant—Remedies Provided by Law

OPTION #4

DEFAULT/REMEDIES. In the event Tenant fails to pay the rent, violates any of the terms of this lease or abandons the premises, then Tenant shall be given 10 days notice by certified mail to cure such default. If Tenant fails to cure such violation Tenant shall be in default under this lease and Landlord shall be entitled to such remedies as provided by law.

If you are familiar with your state's remedies for landlords and they are favorable to your position, you may want to use Option 5:

OPTION #5

DEFAULT/REMEDIES. In the event Tenant defaults under any of the terms of this lease then landlord may proceed as provided by law.

NOTICES

PURPOSE

An address should be available to each party for the giving of legal notices. (*Notice* is an official declaration of a legal action or order.) Cases have been lost because a party used the wrong address in giving a legal notice. If your address changes be sure to give notice by certified mail.

NOTE: *The tenant might not always be using the premises as the legal address for notices, especially if the property is used as a small outlet and the main headquarters is elsewhere.*

NOTICES. Any notice given by the parties to this lease shall be served by certified mail at the following addresses or such other addresses as provided in writing.

Landlord:_____

_____

Tenant:_____

MECHANICS' OR CONSTRUCTION LIENS

PURPOSE
A lien is a claim against a piece of property for which the claimant can take or sell the property. Liens by workers on the property may be called either mechanics' liens or construction liens.

LANDLORD'S
POSITION
The landlord wants to be sure that any work done on the premises does not create a *lien* on the landlord's interest.

TENANT'S
POSITION
The tenant usually has no objection to this clause.

Expanded Clause—No Liens plus Remedies

OPTION #1

MECHANICS' LIENS. Tenant shall have no power or authority to create any lien or permit any lien to attach to the present estate, reversion or other estate of Landlord in the premises herein demised or on the building or other improvements thereon, and all material, men, contractors, artisans, mechanics and laborers and other persons contracting with Tenant with respect to the demised premises or any part thereof, are hereby charged with Notice that they must look to Tenant to secure payment of any bill for work done or material furnished or for any other purpose during the term of this lease. If any such lien attaches, or claim of lien is made, against the demised premises or the building of which said premises are a part, or on the land on which the building is erected and shall not be released by payment, bond or otherwise within thirty (30) days after notice thereof, the Landlord shall have the option of payment or discharging the same and Tenant agrees to reimburse Landlord promptly upon demand.

No Liens by Tenant

OPTION #2

MECHANICS' LIENS. The estate of the Landlord shall not be subject to any liens for improvements contracted for by Tenant.

FIXTURES

PURPOSE
The ownership of *fixtures* installed on the premises should be identified. Fixtures are any items of personal property which are attached to the real property, such as shelving units, ceiling fans, and air conditioning systems.

LANDLORD'S
POSITION
It is usually in the landlord's interest to have the fixtures become part of the property and be left behind.

A tenant may spend $50,000 setting up a restaurant and if this equipment is left behind the landlord will have a much more valuable unit to rent. Because the removal of fixtures often leaves the property in a damaged condition, any removal that is allowed should be conditioned upon repairing the property afterwards.

TENANT'S
POSITION
The tenant would like to take all of his fixtures with him when he moves. However, in most situations tenants cannot expect to take things like common light fixtures and plumbing.

If the tenant owes rent to the landlord when leaving the premises, state law may grant the landlord a lien on the property that was brought onto the premises and the landlord may be able to have the sheriff seize the property from its new location.

In some cases the tenant realizes that the money put into the property cannot be removed. Partitions and built-in fixtures are not worth much once they are removed and the cost of moving them and restoring the premises may be more than they are worth. However, some equipment is readily moveable and very expensive and should not belong to the landlord just because it was brought onto the premises. For protection the lease should be clear about what is to remain on the premises and what can be removed. The tenant might want a special addendum to the lease listing what property can be removed. Whenever fixtures are removed the tenant must fill in any holes in the walls and otherwise restore the property to its original condition.

Fixtures Belong to Landlord

OPTION #1

FIXTURES. Any fixtures installed in the premises shall become the property of the Landlord and such fixtures may not be removed without the specific written consent of Landlord.

Tenant May Remove Some Fixtures

OPTION #2

FIXTURES. Fixtures installed by Tenant on the premises shall remain the property of the Tenant provided the Tenant has not defaulted under this lease and provided that upon any such removal the premises shall be restored to their original condition. Lighting, plumbing, heating and air conditioning equipment, whether or not installed by Tenant shall not be removable, but shall become the property of the Landlord.

Tenant May Remove All Fixtures

OPTION #3

TRADE FIXTURES. All trade fixtures installed by Tenant on the premises shall remain the property of the Tenant provided Tenant has not defaulted under this lease and provided that upon any such removal the premises shall be restored to their original condition.

GUARANTEE

PURPOSE

This clause assures that the lease terms will be fulfilled.

LANDLORD'S
POSITION

If a lease is signed by a corporate tenant, a landlord will usually want a personal guarantee by the owners of the corporation. If such a personal guarantee is not obtained, a corporation with few or no assets can default on the lease without penalty. The landlord who signs a lease with a tenant wants to know that the lease terms will be fulfilled and does not want to worry about the success of the business. A *personal guarantee* of a lease usually means that the tenant personally risks all his assets. If a business has a five year lease at $2000 a month and it closes after a year, the landlord can go after the tenant for the remaining $96,000 in rent.

TENANT'S
POSITION

The tenant usually does not want to risk everything he owns on a business. If the business fails he wants to walk away from it without future liability. The tenant's point of view is that he should not be liable because the landlord can rerent the property to someone else.

In a soft rental market a landlord may be willing to forgo a guarantee if the business looks good. If the tenant refuses to sign a guarantee the landlord might still accept the tenant since rent from a corporation for as long as it lasts is better than an empty unit.

GUARANTEE. In consideration of the acceptance by Landlord of the above Lease the undersigned jointly and severably guarantee full payment and performance of all obligations of Tenant under the Lease.

_____
Guarantor

_____
Guarantor

MISCELLANEOUS CLAUSES FOR THE LANDLORD

PURPOSE In various situations any of the following clauses may be useful in achieving a landlord's objectives or offering extra protections against possible problems.

CLAUSE #1

> HOURS. Tenant shall maintain minimum business hours Monday through Saturday from 10:00 a.m. to 5:00 p.m.

The above clause may help to assure the success of the tenant's business, and also to assure the success of all the stores in a complex by keeping them open at the same times. It does not help attract customers if they find only some of the stores open.

CLAUSE #2

> ABUSE OF PLUMBING. The plumbing facilities shall not be used for any other purpose than that for which they are constructed, and no foreign substance of any kind shall be thrown therein, and the expense of any breakage, stoppage or damage resulting from a violation of this lease shall be borne by the Tenant.

The above clause provides extra warning to the tenant not to abuse the plumbing. It would be useful for tenants which are in a business which might cause damage, such as businesses which use toxic chemicals.

CLAUSE #3

> RELATIONSHIP OF PARTIES. Nothing contained herein shall be deemed or construed by the parties hereto, nor by any third party, as creating the relationship of principal and agent or of partnership or of joint venture between the parties hereto, it being understood and agreed that neither the method of computation of rent, nor any other provision contained herein, nor any acts of the parties herein, shall be deemed to create any relationship between the parties hereto other than the relationship of Landlord and Tenant.

The above clause protects the landlord from any claims that someone might have against a tenant. For example, a person poisoned in a restaurant might want to sue the landlord if the tenant had no money. This clause is usually used in a lease where the rent is based on a percentage of profits, because in such a case the victim could argue that the landlord and tenant were partners.

CLAUSE #4

DANGEROUS MATERIALS. Tenant shall not keep on the premises any item of a dangerous, inflammable, or explosive character that might unreasonably increase the danger of fire on the premises or that might be considered hazardous or extra hazardous by any responsible insurance company.

This clause provides an extra warning to the tenant not to keep anything dangerous on the premises and helps the landlord comply with his insurance policy.

CLAUSE #5

RELEASE OF TENANT. Except as provided in this paragraph, Tenant will not be released on grounds of voluntary or involuntary school withdrawal or transfer, voluntary or involuntary business transfer, marriage, divorce, loss of co-tenants, bad health, voluntary enlistment in the armed services, or any other reason, unless otherwise agreed to in writing by Landlord. However, if Tenant secures a replacement tenant satisfactory to Landlord, Tenant's liability for future rent shall be reduced by the amount of rents actually received from such replacement. If Tenant waives the right to secure a satisfactory replacement, he may secure release of liability for the balance of the lease by paying an amount equal to _____ month's rent, and forfeit his security deposit. All transfer notices must be given at least 30 days in advance in writing. If Tenant is a member of the Armed Forces on extended active duty and receives change-of-duty orders to depart the local area, then Tenant may terminate this lease by giving written 30 day notice providing Tenant is not otherwise in default. In such event, Tenant agrees to furnish Landlord with a copy of the official orders which warrant termination of this lease. (Military orders authorizing base housing DO NOT constitute change-of-duty orders hereunder). In the event of employment transfer by present employer to a location at least 50 miles from local area, Tenant may terminate this agreement by giving written 30 day notice with a notarized copy of the official orders from Tenant's employer. It is agreed that in the event of these transfers, Tenant will waive return of the security deposit but will be financially responsible for the return of the premises in clean condition, etc., per the terms of the security deposit agreement. The employment transfer will only apply if the term of the lease is for 12 months and a minimum of six month's residence has been fulfilled.

Clause 5 is designed to clearly spell out when the tenant may be released from the lease, and what penalty will be imposed. This particular clause relates to a residential lease for premises in an area near a military base, but it may be modified as needed for your situation. Again, be sure to check the laws in your area for any restrictions on such provisions.

MISCELLANEOUS CLAUSES FOR THE TENANT

CLAUSE #1

> RIGHT TO CURE. In the event Tenant shall be in violation of any term under this Lease, Landlord shall send notice of such default by certified mail and Tenant shall have ten (10) days from receipt of such notice to cure the default.

This clause protects the tenant by insuring that if the landlord claims there is a violation, the tenant will be notified in writing and be given a chance to correct it.

The landlord should insist upon the addition of the following sentence to the clause, though it would not be in the tenant's interest:

> In the event the notice is returned unclaimed, the right to such notice shall be waived.

CLAUSE #2

RELEASE OF TENANT. Subject to the provisions of this paragraph, Tenant will be released on grounds of involuntary business or military transfer, or involuntary induction into the armed services. If Tenant secures a replacement tenant satisfactory to Landlord, Tenant's liability for future rent shall be reduced by the amount of rents actually received from such replacement. If Tenant waives the right to secure a satisfactory replacement, he may secure release of liability for the balance of the lease by paying an amount equal to one month's rent. All transfer notices must be given at least 30 days in advance in writing. If Tenant is a member of the Armed Forces on extended active duty and receives change-of-duty orders to depart the local area, then Tenant may terminate this lease by giving written 30 day notice. In such event, Tenant agrees to furnish Landlord with a copy of the official orders which warrant termination of this lease. In the event of employment transfer by present employer to a location at least 20 miles from local area, Tenant may terminate this agreement by giving written 30 day notice with a notarized copy of the official orders from Tenant's employer.

If you have reason to believe that you may be subject to a job or military transfer during the term of the lease, you will want Clause 2 or a similar provision in your lease.

Storage Space Leases 10

Because the financial risk is less for both parties, a lease of storage space facilities can be a lot simpler than for a residence or a business location. For the same reason such leases are usually not covered by many laws. However, some states offer landlords special liens or quick eviction procedures. Owners of such units should check local laws.

Even though the amount involved is small, the landlord still has as a primary goal of wanting to be paid. Therefore the landlord would want to be able to remove the tenant quickly on default and to have a lien against the tenant's property for unpaid rent. The landlord also wants to be sure that no dangerous materials are stored on the premises.

The most important concern of the tenant is that he does not lose his lease (or property) without notice. If, for example a tenant is storing his property while travelling and a rent check is lost in the mail through no fault of the tenant's, then he would not want all of his possessions sold or disposed of.

Ideally a tenant would like to receive notice by certified mail before a default is declared. That way if a check was not received for any reason the tenant could make it up. So, if possible, the tenant should require that such a clause be put in the lease. Like other rentals, storage space leases are usually provided by the landlord and tenants may not have much bargaining power. This might not be acceptable. In such a case the tenant can protect him or herself either by paying rent in advance or having a friend or relative periodically check the status of the rent.

Two simple storage space leases are included in Appendix B. One is for a fixed term and the other for a month-to-month rental. For a more complicated rental a landlord could adapt some of the clauses in Chapters 7 and 9.

For the protection explained above, the tenant could ask the landlord to include the following clause in the lease:

NOTICE. In the event tenant is in default under this lease, tenant shall be given notice by certified mail and allowed 10 days to cure the default.

Glossary

A

abandonment.   Giving up legal rights to a property in such a way as satisfies legal requirements.

access.   The right to enter a rental property.

assessment.   a special tax levied against a piece of property usually based upon some improvement benefiting that property.

assignment.   Transferring the rights and obligations under a lease to another person.

B

bad faith.   Implying or involving fraud or misrepresentation or deception or refusal to fulfill a duty.

C

covenant.   An agreement in an agreement.

D

damages.   Money paid as restitution for a wrongful act.

default.   Committing such acts as violate the terms of a rental agreement.

E

easement.   The legal right of one party to make a certain use of part of the property of another person.

eminent domain.   The right of a government body to take private property upon the payment of just compensation.

eviction.   The legal proceeding to remove a tenant from rental property.

F

fixtures.   Items of personal property which have been attached to real property to be legally considered a part of the real property.

G

grace period.   A period of time during which a party may be allowed to be in violation of an agreement without legal consequences.

guarantee.   An agreement to pay an obligation of another.

H

holdover.   Failing to vacate a property at the end of the legal term of the tenancy.

J

judgment.   A ruling by a court deciding the rights of the parties before it.

judgment-proof.   A situation in which a judgment cannot be collected against a person.

L

landlord.   The owner of a property which has been rented or leased to another person.

land trust.   An arrangement in which one party holds the property of another person in order to keep the ownership confidential (among other reasons).

lease.   An agreement for the use of real property for a set term.

lessee.   The tenant in a lease agreement.

lessor.   The landlord in a lease agreement.

liability.   The responsibility to pay for something such as an injury.

lien.   A claim against a piece or property which is reflected in the title of the property.

N

negligence.   Failure to act in a way required by law.

notice.   Formal notification of a legal situation.

O

option.   A legal right to do something such as extend a lease or buy the property.

ordinance.   A law passed by a city, town or other municipal government.

P

padding.   Adding unnecessary fees to an account.

personal guarantee.   The promise of an individual to be responsible for the debts of a company.

premises.   The area of property which the tenant is entitled to use.

proration.   The division of some expense between two parties usually as of a certain date.

R

recording.   Registering an interest in real property with the government agency in charge of keeping such records.

release.   Relieving someone of a legal obligation.

renewal.   Starting a lease over again upon its expiration.

rent adjustment.   The raising or lowering of rent based upon some external standard.

rent.   The amount of payment required for use of a property which usually does not include other charges such as utilities.

rental agreement.   An agreement for the use of real property, usually on a month-to-month basis.

S

security deposit.   An amount of money paid to a landlord to guarantee the tenant's performance of the terms of the lease.

severability.   The ability to enforce a legal document even if a part of it is declared illegal.

soft market.   A rental marker in which there are many vacancies and few prospective renters.

statute.   A law passed by a state or the federal government.

sublease.   An agreement that a new tenant will lease a unit from an existing tenant.

subordination.   The giving up of legal rights in deference to another party.

surrender.   Giving possession of real property back to the landlord.

T

tenant.   The person renting or leasing a property from another person.

term.   The time period of a rental agreement or lease.

U

unconscionable.   When a provision in a lease shocks the conscience of a judge for him or her to declare it illegal.

undue burden.   An obligation which is more than would be normally necessary.

W

waiver.   The giving up of a legal right.

Z

zoning.   Governmental regulations of the use or real estate.

APPENDIX A
LEAD-BASED PAINT PAMPHLET

This appendix contains the Lead-Based Paint Pamphlet. It gives tips on how to protect yourself and your family. The language contained here is provided by the Environmental Protection Agency, the Consumer Product Safety Commission, and the Department of Housing and Urban Development. This pamphlet is especially important where children will live in the rental because lead-based paint is deadly. See Chapter 4 for more information. You can also find this pamphlet in other formats at:

http://www.hud.gov/lea/leadhelp.html

PROTECT YOUR FAMILY FROM LEAD IN YOUR HOME

Simple Steps To Protect Your Family From Lead Hazards

If you think your home has high levels of lead:

- Get your young children tested for lead, even if they seem healthy.

- Wash children's hands, bottles, pacifiers, and toys often.

- Make sure children eat healthy, low-fat foods.

- Get your home checked for lead hazards.

- Regularly clean floors, window sills, and other surfaces.

- Wipe soil off shoes before entering house.

- Talk to your landlord about fixing surfaces with peeling or chipping paint.

- Take precautions to avoid exposure to lead dust when remodeling or renovating (call 1-800-424-LEAD for guidelines).

- Don't use a belt-sander, propane torch, dry scraper, or dry sandpaper on painted surfaces that may contain lead.

- Don't try to remove lead-based paint yourself.

ARE YOU PLANNING TO BUY, RENT, OR RENOVATE A HOME BUILT BEFORE 1978?

Many houses and apartments built before 1978 have paint that contains lead (called lead-based paint). Lead from paint, chips, and dust can pose serious health hazards if not taken care of properly. By 1996, federal law will require that individuals receive certain information before renting, buying, or renovating pre-1978 housing:

LANDLORDS will have to disclose known information on lead-based paint hazards before leases take effect. Leases will include a federal form about lead-based paint.

SELLERS will have to disclose known information on lead-based paint hazards before selling a house. Sales contracts will include a federal form about lead-based paint in the building. Buyers will have up to 10 days to check for lead hazards.

RENOVATORS will have to give you this pamphlet before starting work.

If you want more information on these requirements, call the National Lead Information Clearinghouse at 1-800-424-LEAD.

This document is in the public domain. It may be reproduced by an individual or organization without permission. Information provided in this booklet is based upon current scientific and technical understanding of the issues presented and is reflective of the jurisdictional boundaries established by the statutes governing the co-authoring agencies. Following the advice given will not necessarily provide complete protection in all situations or against all health hazards that can be caused by lead exposure.

<h1 style="text-align:center">IMPORTANT!</h1>

Lead From Paint, Dust, and Soil Can Be Dangerous If Not Managed Properly

FACT: Lead exposure can harm young children and babies even before they are born.

FACT: Even children that seem healthy can have high levels of lead in their bodies.

FACT: People can get lead in their bodies by breathing or swallowing lead dust, or by eating soil or paint chips with lead in them.

FACT: People have many options for reducing lead hazards. In most cases, lead-based paint that is in good condition is not a hazard.

FACT: Removing lead-based paint improperly can increase the danger to your family.

If you think your home might have lead hazards, read this pamphlet to learn some simple steps to protect your family.

LEAD GETS IN THE BODY IN MANY WAYS

1 out of every 11 children in the United States has dangerous levels of lead in the bloodstream.

Even children who appear healthy can have dangerous levels of lead.

People can get lead in their body if they:

- Put their hands or other objects covered with lead dust in their mouths.

- Eat paint chips or soil that contain lead.

- Breathe in lead dust (especially during renovations that disturb painted surfaces).

Lead is even more dangerous to children than adults because:

- Babies and young children often put their hands and other objects in their mouths. These objects can have lead dust on them.

- Children's growing bodies absorb more lead.

- Children's brains and nervous systems are more sensitive to the damaging effects of lead.

Lead's Effects

If not detected early, children with high levels of lead in their bodies can suffer from:

- Damage to the brain and nervous system

- Behavior and learning problems (such as hyperactivity)

- Slowed growth

- Hearing problems

- Headaches

Lead is also harmful to adults. Adults can suffer from:

- Difficulties during pregnancy

- Other reproductive problems (in both men and women)

- High blood pressure

- Digestive problems

- Nerve disorders

- Memory and concentration problems

- Muscle and joint pain

Lead affects the body in many ways.

CHECKING YOUR FAMILY FOR LEAD

Get your children tested if you think your home has high levels of lead.

A simple blood test can detect high levels of lead. Blood tests are important for:

- Children who are 6 months to 1 year old (6 months if you live in an older home that might have lead in the paint).

- Family members that you think might have high levels of lead.

If your child is older than 1 year, talk to your doctor about whether your child needs testing.

Your doctor or health center can do blood tests. They are inexpensive and sometimes free. Your doctor will explain what the test results mean. Treatment can range from changes in your diet to medication or a hospital stay.

WHERE LEAD-BASED PAINT IS FOUND

In general, the older your home, the more likely it has lead-based paint.

Many homes built before 1978 have lead-based paint. In 1978, the federal government banned lead-based paint from housing. Lead can be found:

- In homes in the city, country, or suburbs.

- In apartments, single-family homes, and both private and public housing.

- Inside and outside of the house.

- In soil around a home. (Soil can pick up lead from exterior paint, or other sources such as past use of leaded gas in cars.)

WHERE LEAD IS LIKELY TO BE A HAZARD

Lead from paint chips, which you can see, and lead dust, which you can't always see, can both be serious hazards.

Lead-based paint that is in good condition is usually not a hazard.

Peeling, chipping, chalking, or cracking lead-based paint is a hazard and needs immediate attention.

Lead-based paint may also be a hazard when found on surfaces that children can chew or that get a lot of wear-and-tear. These areas include:

- Windows and window sills.

- Doors and door frames.

- Stairs, railings, and banisters.

- Porches and fences.

Lead dust can form when lead-based paint is dry scraped, dry sanded, or heated. Dust also forms when painted surfaces bump or rub together. Lead chips and dust can get on surfaces and objects that people touch. Settled lead dust can reenter the air when people vacuum, sweep, or walk through it.

Lead in soil can be a hazard when children play in bare soil or when people bring soil into the house on their shoes. Call your state agency (see below) to find out about soil testing for lead.

CHECKING YOUR HOME FOR LEAD HAZARDS

Just knowing that a home has lead-based paint may not tell you if there is a hazard.

You can get your home checked for lead hazards in one of two ways, or both:

- A paint inspection tells you the lead content of every painted surface in your home. It won't tell you whether the paint is a hazard or how you should deal with it.

- A risk assessment tells you if there are any sources of serious lead exposure (such as peeling paint and lead dust). It also tells you what actions to take to address these hazards.

Have qualified professionals do the work. The federal government is writing standards for inspectors and risk assessors. Some states might already have standards in place. Call your state agency for help with locating qualified professionals in your area (see below).

Trained professionals use a range of methods when checking your home, including:

- Visual inspection of paint condition and location.

- Lab tests of paint samples.

- Surface dust tests.

- A portable x-ray fluorescence machine.

Home test kits for lead are available, but the federal government is still testing their reliability. These tests should not be the only method used before doing renovations or to assure safety.

WHAT YOU CAN DO NOW TO PROTECT YOUR FAMILY

If you suspect that your house has lead hazards, you can take some immediate steps to reduce your family's risk:

- If you rent, notify your landlord of peeling or chipping paint.

- Clean up paint chips immediately.

- Clean floors, window frames, window sills, and other surfaces weekly. Use a mop or sponge with warm water and a general all-purpose cleaner or a cleaner made specifically for lead. REMEMBER: NEVER MIX AMMONIA AND BLEACH PRODUCTS TOGETHER SINCE THEY CAN FORM A DANGEROUS GAS.

- Thoroughly rinse sponges and mop heads after cleaning dirty or dusty areas.

- Wash children's hands often, especially before they eat and before nap time and bed time.

- Keep play areas clean. Wash bottles, pacifiers, toys, and stuffed animals regularly.

- Keep children from chewing window sills or other painted surfaces.

- Clean or remove shoes before entering your home to avoid tracking in lead from soil.

- Make sure children eat nutritious, low-fat meals high in iron and calcium, such as spinach and low-fat dairy products. Children with good diets absorb less lead.

HOW TO SIGNIFICANTLY REDUCE LEAD HAZARDS

Removing lead improperly can increase the hazard to your family by spreading even more lead dust around the house.

Always use a professional who is trained to remove lead hazards safely.

In addition to day-to-day cleaning and good nutrition:

- You can temporarily reduce lead hazards by taking actions like repairing damaged painted surfaces and planting grass to cover soil with high lead levels. These actions (called "interim controls") are not permanent solutions and will not eliminate all risks of exposure.

- To permanently remove lead hazards, you must hire a lead "abatement" contractor. Abatement (or permanent hazard elimination) methods include removing, sealing, or enclosing lead-based paint with special materials. Just painting over the hazard with regular paint is not enough.

Always hire a person with special training for correcting lead problems--someone who knows how to do this work safely and has the proper equipment to clean up thoroughly. If possible, hire a certified lead abatement contractor. Certified contractors will employ qualified workers and follow strict safety rules as set by their state or by the federal government.

Call your state agency (see below) for help with locating qualified contractors in your area and to see if financial assistance is available.

REMODELING OR RENOVATING A HOME WITH LEAD-BASED PAINT

If not conducted properly, certain types of renovations can release lead from paint and dust into the air.

Take precautions before you begin remodeling or renovations that disturb painted surfaces (such as scraping off paint or tearing out walls):

- Have the area tested for lead-based paint.

- Do not use a dry scraper, belt-sander, propane torch, or heat gun to remove lead-based paint. These actions create large amounts of lead dust and fumes. Lead dust can remain in your home long after the work is done.

- Temporarily move your family (especially children and pregnant women) out of the apartment or house until the work is done and the area is properly cleaned. If you can't move your family, at least completely seal off the work area.

- Follow other safety measures to reduce lead hazards. You can find out about other safety measures by calling 1-800-424-LEAD. Ask for the brochure "Reducing Lead Hazards When Remodeling Your Home." This brochure explains what to do before, during, and after renovations.

If you have already completed renovations or remodeling that could have released lead-based paint or dust, get your young children tested and follow the steps outlined above in this brochure.

OTHER SOURCES OF LEAD

While paint, dust, and soil are the most common lead hazards, other lead sources also exist.

- Drinking water. Your home might have plumbing with lead or lead solder. Call your local health department or water supplier to find out about testing your water. You cannot see, smell, or taste lead, and boiling your water will not get rid of lead. If you think your plumbing might have lead in it:

- Use only cold water for drinking and cooking.

- Run water for 15 to 30 seconds before drinking it, especially if you have not used your water for a few hours.

- The job. If you work with lead, you could bring it home on your hands or clothes. Shower and change clothes before coming home. Launder your clothes separately from the rest of your family's.

- Old painted toys and furniture.

- Food and liquids stored in lead crystal or lead-glazed pottery or porcelain.

- Lead smelters or other industries that release lead into the air.

- Hobbies that use lead, such as making pottery or stained glass, or refinishing furniture.

- Folk remedies that contain lead, such as "greta" and "azarcon" used to treat an upset stomach.

FOR MORE INFORMATION

The National Lead Information Center

Call 1-800-LEAD-FYI to learn how to protect children from lead poisoning.

For other information on lead hazards, call the center's clearinghouse at 1-800-424-LEAD. For the hearing impaired, call, TDD 1-800-526-5456 (FAX: 202-659-1192, Internet: EHC@CAIS.COM).

EPA's Safe Drinking Water Hotline

Call 1-800-426-4791 for information about lead in drinking water.

Consumer Product Safety Commission Hotline

To request information on lead in consumer products, or to report an unsafe consumer product or a product-related injury call 1-800-638-2772. (Internet: info@cpsc.gov). For the hearing impaired, call TDD 1-800-638-8270.

STATE HEALTH AND ENVIRONMENTAL AGENCIES

Some cities and states have their own rules for lead-based paint activities. Check with your state agency to see if state or local laws apply to you. Most state agencies can also provide information on finding a lead abatement firm in your area, and on possible sources of financial aid for reducing lead hazards. See http://www.hud.gov/lead for contacts.

EPA REGIONAL OFFICES

Your Regional EPA Office can provide further information regarding regulations and lead protection programs.

EPA Regional Offices

Region 1 (Connecticut, Massachusetts, Maine, New Hampshire, Rhode Island, Vermont)
John F. Kennedy Federal Building
One Congress Street
Boston, MA 02203
(617) 565-3420

Region 2 (New Jersey, New York, Puerto Rico, Virgin Islands) Building 5
2890 Woodbridge Avenue
Edison, NJ 08837-3679
(908) 321-6671

Region 3 (Delaware, Washington DC, Maryland, Pennsylvania, Virginia, West Virginia)
841 Chestnut Building
Philadelphia, PA 19107
(215) 597-9800

Region 4 (Alabama, Florida, Georgia, Kentucky, Mississippi, North Carolina, South Carolina, Tennessee)
61 Alabama St., SW
Atlanta, GA 30303-3104
(404) 562-8956

Region 5 (Illinois, Indiana, Michigan, Minnesota, Ohio, Wisconsin)
77 West Jackson Boulevard
Chicago, IL 60604-3590
(312) 886-6003

Region 6 (Arkansas, Louisiana, New Mexico, Oklahoma, Texas) First Interstate Bank Tower
1445 Ross Avenue, 12th Floor, Suite 1200 Dallas, TX 75202-2733
(214) 665-7244

Region 7 (Iowa, Kansas, Missouri, Nebraska) 726 Minnesota Avenue
Kansas City, KS 66101
(913) 551-7020

Region 8 (Colorado, Montana, North Dakota, South Dakota, Utah, Wyoming)
999 18th Street, Suite 500
Denver, CO 80202-2405
(303) 293-1603

Region 9 (Arizona, California, Hawaii, Nevada) 75 Hawthorne Street
San Francisco, CA 94105
(415) 744-1124

Region 10 (Idaho, Oregon, Washington, Alaska) 1200 Sixth Avenue
Seattle, WA 98101
(206) 553-1200

CPSC REGIONAL OFFICES

Eastern Regional Center
6 World Trade Center
Vesey Street, Room 350
New York, NY 10048
(212) 466-1612

Central Regional Center
230 South Dearborn Street
Room 2944
Chicago, IL 60604-1601
(312) 353-8260

Western Regional Center
600 Harrison Street, Room 245
San Francisco, CA 94107
(415) 744-2966

APPENDIX B
BLANK FORMS

This section includes forms that can be useful in many situations. Keep in mind that these are general forms and not all the clauses may fit your particular situation. You should read them carefully and also read the explanation in this book for each clause. You should weigh the cost of having them reviewed by an attorney against the amount of money you have at risk in the lease. As mentioned in other parts of this book, local law may overrule your lease. You should learn what laws in your area apply to rentals. One helpful step is to obtain copies of leases promulgated by the local bar association or Board of Realtors®

Although you may want to retype your own leases, these forms can be torn out and copied for you use.

Tenant Application

Name_____ Date of Birth _____

Name_____ Date of Birth _____

Soc. Sec. Nos._____

Drivers' License Nos._____

Children & Ages_____

Present Landlord_____ Phone_____

Address _____ How Long?_____

Previous Landlord_____ Phone_____

Address_____

Second Previous Landlord_____ Phone_____

Address_____

Nearest Relative_____ Phone_____

Address_____

Employer_____ Phone_____

Address_____

Second Applicant's Employer_____Phone_____

Address_____

Pets_____

Other persons who will stay at premises for more than one week_____

_____

Bank Name_____Acct. #_____

Bank Name_____Acct. #_____

Have you ever been evicted?_____

Have you ever been in litigation with a landlord?_____

The undersigned hereby attest that the above information is true.

_____

_____

This page intentionally left blank.

House Lease

LANDLORD:_____ TENANT:_____

_____ _____

PROPERTY:_____

IN CONSIDERATION of the mutual covenants and agreements herein contained, Landlord hereby leases to Tenant and Tenant hereby leases from Landlord the above-described property together with any personal property listed on "Schedule A" attached hereto, under the following terms and conditions:

1. TERM. This lease shall be for a term of _____ beginning _____, _____ and ending _____, _____.

2. RENT. The rent shall be $_____ per _____ and shall be due on or before the _____ day of each _____. In the event the full amount of rent is not received on the due date, a late charge of $_____ shall be due. In the event a check is returned unpaid or an eviction notice must be posted, Tenant agrees to pay a $_____ charge.

3. PAYMENT. Payment must be received by Landlord on or before the due date at the following address: _____ or such place as designated by Landlord in writing. Tenant understands that this may require early mailing. In the event a check is returned unpaid, Landlord may require cash or certified funds.

4. DEFAULT. In the event Tenant defaults under any term of this lease, Landlord may recover possession as provided by law and seek monetary damages.

5. SECURITY. Tenant shall pay Landlord the sum of $_____ as the last month's rent under this lease, plus $_____ as security deposit. In the event Tenant terminates the lease prior to its expiration date, said amounts are non-refundable as a charge for Landlord's trouble in finding a new tenant, but Landlord reserves the right to seek additional damages if they exceed the amount of deposits.

6. UTILITIES. Tenant agrees to pay all utility charges on the property except: _____ _____.

7. MAINTENANCE. Tenant has examined the property, acknowledges it to be in good repair and in consideration of the reduced rent, Tenant agrees to be responsible for and to promptly complete all maintenance to the premises.

8. LOCKS. If Tenant adds or changes locks on the premises, Landlord shall be given copies of the keys. Landlord shall at all times have keys for access to the premises in case of emergencies.

9. ASSIGNMENT. Tenant may not assign this lease or sublet any part of the premises without Landlord's written consent, which consent shall be at Landlord's sole discretion.

10. USE. Tenant agrees to use the premises for residential purposes only and not for any illegal purpose or any purpose which will increase the rate of insurance. Tenant further agrees not to violate any zoning laws or subdivision restrictions or to engage in any activity which would injure the premises or constitute a nuisance to the neighbors or Landlord.

11. LAWN. Tenant shall be responsible for maintaining the lawn and shrubbery on the premises at Tenant's expense and for any damages caused by his neglect or abuse thereof.

12. LIABILITY. Tenant agrees to hold Landlord harmless from any and all claims for damages occurring on the premises, and to be solely responsible for insuring Tenant's own possessions on the premises.

13. ACCESS. Landlord reserves the right to enter the premises for the purposes of inspection, repair, or showing to prospective tenants or purchasers.

14. PETS. No pets shall be allowed on the premises except: _____ and there shall be a non-refundable $_____ pet deposit. Landlord reserves the right to revoke consent if pet becomes a nuisance.

15. OCCUPANCY. The premises shall not be occupied by more than _____ persons.

16. TENANT'S APPLIANCES. Tenant agrees not to use any heaters, fixtures or appliances drawing excessive current without the written consent of the Landlord.

17. PARKING. Tenant agrees that no parking is allowed on the premises except:_____ _____. Campers, trailers, boats, recreational vehicles or inoperable vehicles shall not be stored on the premises without the written consent of the Landlord.

18. FURNISHINGS. Tenant acknowledges receipt of the items listed on "Schedule A" attached hereto and agrees to return them in good condition at the end of this lease.

19. ALTERATIONS AND IMPROVEMENTS. Tenant shall make no alterations or improvements to the premises (including paint) without the written consent of the Landlord and any such alterations or improvements shall become the property of the Landlord unless otherwise agreed in writing.

20. ENTIRE AGREEMENT. This lease constitutes the entire agreement between the parties and may not be modified except in writing signed by both parties.

21. HARASSMENT. Tenant shall not do any acts to intentionally harass the Landlord or other tenants.

22. ATTORNEY'S FEES. In the event Landlord must use the services of an attorney to enforce this agreement, Tenant shall pay Landlord's attorney's fees.

23. SEVERABILITY. In the event any section of this agreement shall be held to be invalid, all remaining provisions shall remain in full force and effect.

24. RECORDING. This lease shall not be recorded in any public records.

25. WAIVER. Any failure by Landlord to exercise any rights under this agreement shall not constitute a waiver of Landlord's rights.

26. ABANDONMENT. In the event Tenant abandons the property prior to the expiration of this lease, Landlord may relet the premises and hold Tenant liable for any costs, lost rent or damage to the premises. Landlord may dispose of any personal property abandoned by Tenant.

27. SUBORDINATION. Tenant's interest in the premises shall be subordinate to any encumbrances now or hereafter placed on the premises, to any advances made under such encumbrances, and to any extensions or renewals thereof. Tenant agrees to sign any documents indicating such subordination which may be required by lenders.

28. SURRENDER OF PREMISES. At the expiration of the term of this lease, Tenant shall immediately surrender possession of the premises in as good condition as at the start of this lease. The Tenant shall turn over to Landlord all keys to the premises, including keys made by Tenant or Tenant's agents.

29. HOLDOVER BY TENANT. If Tenant fails to deliver possession of the premises to Landlord at the expiration of this lease, the tenancy shall still be governed by this lease on a month-to-month basis. If such holdover is without the consent of the Landlord, Tenant shall be liable for double the monthly rent for each month or fraction thereof.

30. DAMAGE TO PREMISES. In the event the premises are damaged or destroyed by fire or other casualty or are declared uninhabitable by a governmental authority, Landlord may terminate this lease or may repair the premises.

31. PEST CONTROL. Tenant agrees to be responsible for pest control and extermination services on the premises, and to keep the premises clean and sanitary to avoid such problems. Tenant shall notify Landlord immediately of any evidence of termites. Landlord shall not be responsible to provide living arrangements for Tenant in the event the premises must be vacated for termite or other pest control treatment.

32. LIENS. The estate of the Landlord shall not be subject to any liens for improvements contracted by Tenant.

33. WATERBEDS. In the event Tenant uses a flotation type bedding device on the premises, Tenant shall maintain an insurance policy of at least $_____ to cover damages from such device and shall list Landlord as a named insured on said policy.

34. MISCELLANEOUS PROVISIONS. _____
_____.

WITNESS the hands and seals of the parties hereto as of this _____ day of _____, _____.

LANDLORD: TENANT:

_____   _____

_____   _____

HOUSE RENTAL AGREEMENT

LANDLORD:_____   TENANT:_____

_____   _____

PROPERTY:_____

IN CONSIDERATION of the mutual covenants and agreements herein contained, Landlord hereby leases to Tenant and Tenant hereby leases from Landlord the above-described property together with any personal property listed on "Schedule A" attached hereto, under the following terms and conditions:

1. TERM. This rental agreement shall be for a month-to-month tenancy which may be cancelled by either party upon giving notice to the other party at least 30 days prior to the end of the month.

2. RENT. The rent shall be $_____ per _____ and shall be due on or before the _____ day of each _____. In the event the full amount of rent is not received on the due date, a late charge of $_____ shall be due. In the event a check is returned unpaid or an eviction notice must be posted, Tenant agrees to pay a $_____ charge.

3. PAYMENT. Payment must be received by Landlord on or before the due date at the following address: _____ or such place as designated by Landlord in writing. Tenant understands that this may require early mailing. In the event a check is returned unpaid, Landlord may require cash or certified funds.

4. DEFAULT. In the event Tenant defaults under any term of this lease, Landlord may recover possession as provided by law and seek monetary damages.

5. SECURITY. Tenant shall pay Landlord the sum of $_____ as the last month's rent under this lease, plus $_____ as security deposit. In the event Tenant terminates the lease prior to its expiration date, said amounts are non-refundable as a charge for Landlord's trouble in securing a new tenant, but Landlord reserves the right to seek additional damages if they exceed the amounts of deposits.

6. UTILITIES. Tenant agrees to pay all utility charges on the property except: _____ _____.

7. MAINTENANCE. Tenant has examined the property, acknowledges it to be in good repair and in consideration of the reduced rent, Tenant agrees to be responsible for and to promptly complete all maintenance to the premises.

8. LOCKS. If Tenant adds or changes locks on the premises, Landlord shall be given copies of the keys. Landlord shall at all times have keys for access to the premises in case of emergencies.

9. ASSIGNMENT. Tenant may not assign this lease or sublet any part of the premises without Landlord's written consent, which consent shall be at Landlord's sole discretion.

10. USE. Tenant agrees to use the premises for residential purposes only and not for any illegal purpose or any purpose which will increase the rate of insurance. Tenant further agrees not to violate any zoning laws or subdivision restrictions or to engage in any activity which would injure the premises or constitute a nuisance to the neighbors or Landlord.

11. LAWN. Tenant shall be responsible for maintaining the lawn and shrubbery on the premises at Tenant's expense and for any damages caused by his neglect or abuse thereof.

12. LIABILITY. Tenant agrees to hold Landlord harmless from any and all claims for damages occurring on the premises, and to be solely responsible for insuring Tenant's own possessions on the premises.

13. ACCESS. Landlord reserves the right to enter the premises for the purposes of inspection, repair, or showing to prospective tenants or purchasers.

14. PETS. No pets shall be allowed on the premises except: _____ and there shall be a non-refundable $_____ pet deposit. Landlord reserves the right to revoke consent if pet becomes a nuisance.

15. OCCUPANCY. The premises shall not be occupied by more than _____ persons.

16. TENANT'S APPLIANCES. Tenant agrees not to use any heaters, fixtures or appliances drawing excessive current without the written consent of the Landlord.

17. PARKING. Tenant agrees that no parking is allowed on the premises except:_____ _____. Campers, trailers, boats, recreational vehicles or inoperable vehicles shall not be stored on the premises without the written consent of the Landlord.

18. FURNISHINGS. Tenant acknowledges receipt of the items listed on "Schedule A" attached hereto and agrees to return them in good condition at the end of this lease.

19. ALTERATIONS AND IMPROVEMENTS. Tenant shall make no alterations or improvements to the premises (including paint) without the written consent of the Landlord and any such alterations or improvements shall become the property of the Landlord unless otherwise agreed in writing.

20. ENTIRE AGREEMENT. This lease constitutes the entire agreement between the parties and may not be modified except in writing signed by both parties.

21. HARASSMENT. Tenant shall not do any acts to intentionally harass the Landlord or other tenants.

22. ATTORNEY'S FEES. In the event Landlord must use the services of an attorney to enforce this agreement, Tenant shall pay Landlord's attorney's fees.

23. SEVERABILITY. In the event any section of this agreement shall be held to be invalid, all remaining provisions shall remain in full force and effect.

24. RECORDING. This lease shall not be recorded in any public records.

25. WAIVER. Any failure by Landlord to exercise any rights under this agreement shall not constitute a waiver of Landlord's rights.

26. ABANDONMENT. In the event Tenant abandons the property prior to the expiration of this lease, Landlord may relet the premises and hold Tenant liable for any costs, lost rent or damage to the premises. Landlord may dispose of any personal property abandoned by Tenant.

27. SUBORDINATION. Tenant's interest in the premises shall be subordinate to any encumbrances now or hereafter placed on the premises, to any advances made under such encumbrances, and to any extensions or renewals thereof. Tenant agrees to sign any documents indicating such subordination which may be required by lenders.

28. SURRENDER OF PREMISES. At the expiration of the term of this lease, Tenant shall immediately surrender possession of the premises in as good condition as at the start of this lease. The Tenant shall turn over to Landlord all keys to the premises, including keys made by Tenant or Tenant's agents.

29. HOLDOVER BY TENANT. If Tenant fails to deliver possession of the premises to Landlord at the expiration of this lease, the tenancy shall still be governed by this lease on a month-to-month basis. If such holdover is without the consent of the Landlord, Tenant shall be liable for double the monthly rent for each month or fraction thereof.

30. DAMAGE TO PREMISES. In the event the premises are damaged or destroyed by fire or other casualty or are declared uninhabitable by a governmental authority, Landlord may terminate this lease or may repair the premises.

31. PEST CONTROL. Tenant agrees to be responsible for pest control and extermination services on the premises, and to keep the premises clean and sanitary to avoid such problems. Tenant shall notify Landlord immediately of any evidence of termites. Landlord shall not be responsible to provide living arrangements for Tenant in the event the premises must be vacated for termite or other pest control treatment.

32. LIENS. The estate of the Landlord shall not be subject to any liens for improvements contracted by Tenant.

33. WATERBEDS. In the event Tenant uses a flotation type bedding device on the premises, Tenant shall maintain an insurance policy of at least $_____ to cover damages from such device and shall list Landlord as a named insured on said policy.

34. MISCELLANEOUS PROVISIONS. _____
_____.

WITNESS the hands and seals of the parties hereto as of this _____ day of _____,
_____.

LANDLORD: TENANT:

_____   _____

_____   _____

House Rental Agreement

LANDLORD:_____   TENANT:_____

_____   _____

PROPERTY:_____

IN CONSIDERATION of the mutual covenants and agreements herein contained, Landlord hereby leases to Tenant and Tenant hereby leases from Landlord the above-described property together with any personal property listed on "Schedule A" attached hereto, under the following terms and conditions:

    1. TERM. This rental agreement shall be for a month-to-month tenancy which may be cancelled by either party upon giving notice to the other party at least 30 days prior to the end of the month.

    2. RENT. The rent shall be $_____ per _____ and shall be due on or before the _____ day of each _____. In the event the full amount of rent is not received on the due date, a late charge of $_____ shall be due. In the event a check is returned unpaid or an eviction notice must be posted, Tenant agrees to pay a $_____ charge.

    3. PAYMENT. Payment must be received by Landlord on or before the due date at the following address: _____ or such place as designated by Landlord in writing. Tenant understands that this may require early mailing. In the event a check is returned unpaid, Landlord may require cash or certified funds.

    4. DEFAULT. In the event Tenant defaults under any term of this lease, Landlord may recover possession as provided by law and seek monetary damages.

    5. SECURITY. Tenant shall pay Landlord the sum of $_____ as the last month's rent under this lease, plus $_____ as security deposit. In the event Tenant terminates the lease prior to its expiration date, said amounts are non-refundable as a charge for Landlord's trouble in securing a new tenant, but Landlord reserves the right to seek additional damages if they exceed the amounts of deposits.

    6. UTILITIES. Tenant agrees to pay all utility charges on the property except: _____ _____.

    7. MAINTENANCE. Tenant has examined the property, acknowledges it to be in good repair and in consideration of the reduced rent, Tenant agrees to be responsible for and to promptly complete all maintenance to the premises.

    8. LOCKS. If Tenant adds or changes locks on the premises, Landlord shall be given copies of the keys. Landlord shall at all times have keys for access to the premises in case of emergencies.

    9. ASSIGNMENT. Tenant may not assign this lease or sublet any part of the premises without Landlord's written consent, which consent shall be at Landlord's sole discretion.

    10. USE. Tenant agrees to use the premises for residential purposes only and not for any illegal purpose or any purpose which will increase the rate of insurance. Tenant further agrees not to violate any zoning laws or subdivision restrictions or to engage in any activity which would injure the premises or constitute a nuisance to the neighbors or Landlord.

    11. LAWN. Tenant shall be responsible for maintaining the lawn and shrubbery on the premises at Tenant's expense and for any damages caused by his neglect or abuse thereof.

    12. LIABILITY. Tenant agrees to hold Landlord harmless from any and all claims for damages occurring on the premises, and to be solely responsible for insuring Tenant's own possessions on the premises.

    13. ACCESS. Landlord reserves the right to enter the premises for the purposes of inspection, repair, or showing to prospective tenants or purchasers.

    14. PETS. No pets shall be allowed on the premises except: _____ and there shall be a non-refundable $_____ pet deposit. Landlord reserves the right to revoke consent if pet becomes a nuisance.

    15. OCCUPANCY. The premises shall not be occupied by more than _____ persons.

    16. TENANT'S APPLIANCES. Tenant agrees not to use any heaters, fixtures or appliances drawing excessive current without the written consent of the Landlord.

    17. PARKING. Tenant agrees that no parking is allowed on the premises except:_____ _____. Campers, trailers, boats, recreational vehicles or inoperable vehicles shall not be stored on the premises without the written consent of the Landlord.

    18. FURNISHINGS. Tenant acknowledges receipt of the items listed on "Schedule A" attached hereto and agrees to return them in good condition at the end of this lease.

173

19. ALTERATIONS AND IMPROVEMENTS. Tenant shall make no alterations or improvements to the premises (including paint) without the written consent of the Landlord and any such alterations or improvements shall become the property of the Landlord unless otherwise agreed in writing.

20. ENTIRE AGREEMENT. This lease constitutes the entire agreement between the parties and may not be modified except in writing signed by both parties.

21. HARASSMENT. Tenant shall not do any acts to intentionally harass the Landlord or other tenants.

22. ATTORNEY'S FEES. In the event Landlord must use the services of an attorney to enforce this agreement, Tenant shall pay Landlord's attorney's fees.

23. SEVERABILITY. In the event any section of this agreement shall be held to be invalid, all remaining provisions shall remain in full force and effect.

24. RECORDING. This lease shall not be recorded in any public records.

25. WAIVER. Any failure by Landlord to exercise any rights under this agreement shall not constitute a waiver of Landlord's rights.

26. ABANDONMENT. In the event Tenant abandons the property prior to the expiration of this lease, Landlord may relet the premises and hold Tenant liable for any costs, lost rent or damage to the premises. Landlord may dispose of any personal property abandoned by Tenant.

27. SUBORDINATION. Tenant's interest in the premises shall be subordinate to any encumbrances now or hereafter placed on the premises, to any advances made under such encumbrances, and to any extensions or renewals thereof. Tenant agrees to sign any documents indicating such subordination which may be required by lenders.

28. SURRENDER OF PREMISES. At the expiration of the term of this lease, Tenant shall immediately surrender possession of the premises in as good condition as at the start of this lease. The Tenant shall turn over to Landlord all keys to the premises, including keys made by Tenant or Tenant's agents.

29. HOLDOVER BY TENANT. If Tenant fails to deliver possession of the premises to Landlord at the expiration of this lease, the tenancy shall still be governed by this lease on a month-to-month basis. If such holdover is without the consent of the Landlord, Tenant shall be liable for double the monthly rent for each month or fraction thereof.

30. DAMAGE TO PREMISES. In the event the premises are damaged or destroyed by fire or other casualty or are declared uninhabitable by a governmental authority, Landlord may terminate this lease or may repair the premises.

31. PEST CONTROL. Tenant agrees to be responsible for pest control and extermination services on the premises, and to keep the premises clean and sanitary to avoid such problems. Tenant shall notify Landlord immediately of any evidence of termites. Landlord shall not be responsible to provide living arrangements for Tenant in the event the premises must be vacated for termite or other pest control treatment.

32. LIENS. The estate of the Landlord shall not be subject to any liens for improvements contracted by Tenant.

33. WATERBEDS. In the event Tenant uses a flotation type bedding device on the premises, Tenant shall maintain an insurance policy of at least $_____ to cover damages from such device and shall list Landlord as a named insured on said policy.

34. MISCELLANEOUS PROVISIONS. _____
_____.

WITNESS the hands and seals of the parties hereto as of this _____ day of _____,
_____.

LANDLORD: TENANT:

_____   _____

_____   _____

APARTMENT LEASE

LANDLORD:_____   TENANT:_____

_____   _____

PROPERTY:_____

IN CONSIDERATION of the mutual covenants and agreements herein contained, Landlord hereby leases to Tenant and Tenant hereby leases from Landlord the above-described property together with any personal property listed on "Schedule A" attached hereto, under the following terms and conditions:

1. TERM. This lease shall be for a term of _____ beginning _____, _____ and ending _____, _____.

2. RENT. The rent shall be $_____ per _____ and shall be due on or before the _____ day of each _____. In the event the full amount of rent is not received on the due date, a late charge of $_____ shall be due. In the event a check is returned unpaid or an eviction notice must be posted, Tenant agrees to pay a $_____ charge.

3. PAYMENT. Payment must be received by Landlord on or before the due date at the following address: _____ or such place as designated by Landlord in writing. Tenant understands that this may require early mailing. In the event a check is returned unpaid, Landlord may require cash or certified funds.

4. DEFAULT. In the event Tenant defaults under any term of this lease, Landlord may recover possession as provided by law and seek monetary damages.

5. SECURITY. Tenant shall pay Landlord the sum of $_____ as security for the performance of this lease. Said amount shall not be used as rent.

6. UTILITIES. Tenant agrees to pay all utility charges on the property except: _____ _____.

7. MAINTENANCE. Tenant has examined the property, acknowledges it to be in good repair and agrees to inform Landlord promptly of any maintenance problems. Tenant agrees to keep the premises in clean and sanitary condition. In the event damage has been done by Tenant or Tenant's guests, either intentionally or negligently, Tenant shall pay for such repairs within ten days.

8. LOCKS. If Tenant adds or changes locks on the premises, Landlord shall be given copies of the keys. Landlord shall at all times have keys for access to the premises in case of emergencies.

9. ASSIGNMENT. Tenant may not assign this lease or sublet any part of the premises without Landlord's written consent, which consent shall be at Landlord's sole discretion.

10. USE. Tenant agrees to use the premises for residential purposes only and not for any illegal purpose or any purpose which will increase the rate of insurance. Tenant further agrees not to violate any zoning laws or subdivision restrictions or to engage in any activity which would injure the premises or constitute a nuisance to the neighbors or Landlord.

11. CONDOMINIUM. In the event the premises are a condominium unit, Tenant agrees to abide by all applicable rules and regulations. Maintenance and recreation fees are to be paid by _____. This lease is subject to the approval of the condominium association and Tenant agrees to pay any fee necessary for such approval.

12. LIABILITY. Tenant agrees to hold Landlord harmless from any and all claims for damages occurring on the premises, and to be solely responsible for insuring Tenant's own possessions on the premises.

13. ACCESS. Landlord reserves the right to enter the premises for the purposes of inspection, repair, or showing to prospective tenants or purchasers.

14. PETS. No pets shall be allowed on the premises except: _____ and there shall be a non-refundable $_____ pet deposit. Landlord reserves the right to revoke consent if pet becomes a nuisance.

15. OCCUPANCY. The premises shall not be occupied by more than _____ persons.

16. TENANT'S APPLIANCES. Tenant agrees not to use any heaters, fixtures or appliances drawing excessive current without the written consent of the Landlord.

17. PARKING. Tenant agrees that no parking is allowed on the premises except:_____

_____. Campers, trailers, boats, recreational vehicles or inoperable vehicles shall not be stored on the premises without the written consent of the Landlord.

18. FURNISHINGS. Tenant acknowledges receipt of the items listed on "Schedule A" attached hereto and agrees to return them in good condition at the end of this lease.

19. ALTERATIONS AND IMPROVEMENTS. Tenant shall make no alterations or improvements to the premises (including paint) without the written consent of the Landlord and any such alterations or improvements shall become the property of the Landlord unless otherwise agreed to in writing.

20. ENTIRE AGREEMENT. This lease constitutes the entire agreement between the parties and may not be modified except in writing signed by both parties.

21. HARASSMENT. Tenant shall not do any acts to intentionally harass the Landlord or other tenants.

22. ATTORNEY'S FEES. In the event Landlord must use the services of an attorney to enforce this agreement, Tenant shall pay Landlord's attorney's fees.

23. SEVERABILITY. In the event any section of this agreement shall be held to be invalid, all remaining provisions shall remain in full force and effect.

24. RECORDING. This lease shall not be recorded in any public records.

25. WAIVER. Any failure by Landlord to exercise any rights under this agreement shall not constitute a waiver of Landlord's rights.

26. ABANDONMENT. In the event Tenant abandons the property prior to the expiration of this lease, Landlord may relet the premises and hold Tenant liable for any costs, lost rent or damage to the premises. Landlord may dispose of any personal property abandoned by Tenant.

27. SUBORDINATION. Tenant's interest in the premises shall be subordinate to any encumbrances now or hereafter placed on the premises, to any advances made under such encumbrances, and to any extensions or renewals thereof. Tenant agrees to sign any documents indicating such subordination which may be required by lenders.

28. SURRENDER OF PREMISES. At the expiration of the term of this lease, Tenant shall immediately surrender possession of the premises in as good condition as at the start of this lease. The Tenant shall turn over to Landlord all keys to the premises, including keys made by Tenant or Tenant's agents.

29. HOLDOVER BY TENANT. If Tenant fails to deliver possession of the premises to Landlord at the expiration of this lease, the tenancy shall still be governed by this lease on a month-to-month basis. If such holdover is without the consent of the Landlord, Tenant shall be liable for double the monthly rent for each month or fraction thereof.

30. DAMAGE TO PREMISES. In the event the premises are damaged or destroyed by fire or other casualty or are declared uninhabitable by a governmental authority, Landlord may terminate this lease or may repair the premises.

31. LIENS. The estate of the Landlord shall not be subject to any liens for improvements contracted by Tenant.

32. WATERBEDS. In the event Tenant uses a flotation type bedding device on the premises, Tenant shall maintain an insurance policy of at least $_____ to cover damages from such device and shall list Landlord as a named insured on said policy.

33. MISCELLANEOUS PROVISIONS. _____
_____.

WITNESS the hands and seals of the parties hereto as of this _____ day of _____, _____.

LANDLORD: TENANT:

_____   _____

_____   _____

176

APARTMENT RENTAL AGREEMENT

LANDLORD:_____   TENANT:_____

_____   _____

PROPERTY:_____

IN CONSIDERATION of the mutual covenants and agreements herein contained, Landlord hereby leases to Tenant and Tenant hereby leases from Landlord the above-described property together with any personal property listed on "Schedule A" attached hereto, under the following terms and conditions:

1. TERM. This rental agreement shall be for a month-to-month tenancy which may be cancelled by either party upon giving notice to the other party at least 30 days prior to the end of the month.

2. RENT. The rent shall be $_____ per _____ and shall be due on or before the _____ day of each _____. In the event the full amount of rent is not received on the due date, a late charge of $_____ shall be due. In the event a check is returned unpaid or an eviction notice must be posted, Tenant agrees to pay a $_____ charge.

3. PAYMENT. Payment must be received by Landlord on or before the due date at the following address: _____ or such place as designated by Landlord in writing. Tenant understands that this may require early mailing. In the event a check is returned unpaid, Landlord may require cash or certified funds.

4. DEFAULT. In the event Tenant defaults under any term of this lease, Landlord may recover possession as provided by law and seek monetary damages.

5. SECURITY. Tenant shall pay Landlord the sum of $_____ as security for the performance of this lease. Said amount shall not be used as rent.

6. UTILITIES. Tenant agrees to pay all utility charges on the property except: _____ _____.

7. MAINTENANCE. Tenant has examined the property, acknowledges it to be in good repair and agrees to inform Landlord promptly of any maintenance problems. Tenant agrees to keep the premises in clean and sanitary condition. In the event damage has been done by Tenant or Tenant's guests, either intentionally or negligently, Tenant shall pay for such repairs within ten days.

8. LOCKS. If Tenant adds or changes locks on the premises, Landlord shall be given copies of the keys. Landlord shall at all times have keys for access to the premises in case of emergencies.

9. ASSIGNMENT. Tenant may not assign this lease or sublet any part of the premises without Landlord's written consent, which consent shall be at Landlord's sole discretion.

10. USE. Tenant agrees to use the premises for residential purposes only and not for any illegal purpose or any purpose which will increase the rate of insurance. Tenant further agrees not to violate any zoning laws or subdivision restrictions or to engage in any activity which would injure the premises or constitute a nuisance to the neighbors or Landlord.

11. CONDOMINIUM. In the event the premises are a condominium unit, Tenant agrees to abide by all applicable rules and regulations. Maintenance and recreation fees are to be paid by _____. This lease is subject to the approval of the condominium association and Tenant agrees to pay any fee necessary for such approval.

12. LIABILITY. Tenant agrees to hold Landlord harmless from any and all claims for damages occurring on the premises, and to be solely responsible for insuring Tenant's own possessions on the premises.

13. ACCESS. Landlord reserves the right to enter the premises for the purposes of inspection, repair, or showing to prospective tenants or purchasers.

14. PETS. No pets shall be allowed on the premises except: _____ and there shall be a non-refundable $_____ pet deposit. Landlord reserves the right to revoke consent if pet becomes a nuisance.

15. OCCUPANCY. The premises shall not be occupied by more than _____ persons.

16. TENANT'S APPLIANCES. Tenant agrees not to use any heaters, fixtures or appliances drawing excessive current without the written consent of the Landlord.

17. PARKING. Tenant agrees that no parking is allowed on the premises except:_____

_____. Campers, trailers, boats, recreational vehicles or inoperable vehicles shall not be stored on the premises without the written consent of the Landlord.

18. FURNISHINGS. Tenant acknowledges receipt of the items listed on "Schedule A" attached hereto and agrees to return them in good condition at the end of this lease.

19. ALTERATIONS AND IMPROVEMENTS. Tenant shall make no alterations or improvements to the premises (including paint) without the written consent of the Landlord and any such alterations or improvements shall become the property of the Landlord unless otherwise agreed to in writing.

20. ENTIRE AGREEMENT. This lease constitutes the entire agreement between the parties and may not be modified except in writing signed by both parties.

21. HARASSMENT. Tenant shall not do any acts to intentionally harass the Landlord or other tenants.

22. ATTORNEY'S FEES. In the event Landlord must use the services of an attorney to enforce this agreement, Tenant shall pay Landlord's attorney's fees.

23. SEVERABILITY. In the event any section of this agreement shall be held to be invalid, all remaining provisions shall remain in full force and effect.

24. RECORDING. This lease shall not be recorded in any public records.

25. WAIVER. Any failure by Landlord to exercise any rights under this agreement shall not constitute a waiver of Landlord's rights.

26. ABANDONMENT. In the event Tenant abandons the property prior to the expiration of this lease, Landlord may relet the premises and hold Tenant liable for any costs, lost rent or damage to the premises. Landlord may dispose of any personal property abandoned by Tenant.

27. SUBORDINATION. Tenant's interest in the premises shall be subordinate to any encumbrances now or hereafter placed on the premises, to any advances made under such encumbrances, and to any extensions or renewals thereof. Tenant agrees to sign any documents indicating such subordination which may be required by lenders.

28. SURRENDER OF PREMISES. At the expiration of the term of this lease, Tenant shall immediately surrender possession of the premises in as good condition as at the start of this lease. The Tenant shall turn over to Landlord all keys to the premises, including keys made by Tenant or Tenant's agents.

29. HOLDOVER BY TENANT. If Tenant fails to deliver possession of the premises to Landlord at the expiration of this lease, the tenancy shall still be governed by this lease on a month-to-month basis. If such holdover is without the consent of the Landlord, Tenant shall be liable for double the monthly rent for each month or fraction thereof.

30. DAMAGE TO PREMISES. In the event the premises are damaged or destroyed by fire or other casualty or are declared uninhabitable by a governmental authority, Landlord may terminate this lease or may repair the premises.

31. LIENS. The estate of the Landlord shall not be subject to any liens for improvements contracted by Tenant.

32. WATERBEDS. In the event Tenant uses a flotation type bedding device on the premises, Tenant shall maintain an insurance policy of at least $_____ to cover damages from such device and shall list Landlord as a named insured on said policy.

33. MISCELLANEOUS PROVISIONS. _____
_____.

WITNESS the hands and seals of the parties hereto as of this _____ day of _____, _____.

LANDLORD: TENANT:

_____   _____

_____   _____

COMMERCIAL LEASE

LANDLORD:_____   TENANT:_____

_____   _____

    IN CONSIDERATION of the mutual covenants and conditions herein contained, Landlord leases to Tenant and Tenant leases from Landlord the property described under the following terms and conditions:

    1. PREMISES. The premises leased by Tenant consist of a _____ of approximately _____ square feet located at _____ as measured from exterior surfaces of outside walls and center lines of dividing walls including all plumbing, electrical, sewerage, heating, air conditioning and other utilities fixtures, lines, equipment, pipes, cables and posts thereof together with the common use with other Tenants of all parking, roads and walkways and other public areas.

    2. TERM. The term of this lease shall be for a period of _____ months commencing at 12:01 a.m. on _____, _____, and ending at midnight on _____, _____.

    3. RENT. The base rent for the first year of this lease shall be $_____ per month. For the second and each subsequent year under this lease the rent shall be increased by the same percentage increase as the of the "Consumer Price Index - All Items - U. S. City Average" for the previous twelve months. In addition to the base rent the Tenant shall pay _____% of the charges for real estate taxes, utilities and maintenance of the common areas, together with any sales or use tax due for the rental of the premises.

    4. RENEWAL. Providing that Tenant is not in default under any term of this lease, Tenant is hereby given an option to renew this lease for a term of _____ years. The base rent for the first year of the renewal shall be the amount of rent for the previous year plus the percentage increase of the of the "Consumer Price Index - All Items - U. S. City Average." (CPI) for the previous twelve months. For each subsequent year the rent shall increase according to the CPI. Tenant shall give Landlord written notice sixty (60) days prior to the end of this lease of intent to renew.

    5. PAYMENT OF RENT. Payments must be received by the Landlord on or before the due date at the following address: _____ or such other place as designated by Landlord in writing. Payments sent through the mail are at Tenant's risk, and Tenant acknowledges that early mailing may be required for rent to be received on time. Landlord reserves the right, at any time, to require that the rent be paid in the form of cash or certified funds.

    6. SECURITY. Tenant shall pay to Landlord the sum of $_____ as last month's rent under this lease, plus $_____ as security deposit.

    7. UTILITIES. The Tenant shall be responsible for all charges for electricity, gas, water, sewer or other utilities supplied to the premises. Any such charges not billed directly to Tenant shall be reimbursed to Landlord each month upon presentation of a statement.

    8. MAINTENANCE & REPAIR. The Landlord shall keep the foundation, outer walls and roof of the premises and the common areas in good repair, except that Landlord shall not be liable for any repairs occasioned by the acts of Tenant, its agents or employees. Tenant shall be responsible for maintenance and repair to the inside of the premises including heating and cooling systems, electrical, plumbing, machinery, hardware, doors, windows, screens and painting. All such repairs shall be made with materials and workmanship equivalent to the original. Tenant shall be responsible for extermination service to the premises.

    9. ALTERATIONS & IMPROVEMENTS. Tenant shall make no alterations, decoration, additions or improvements in or to the premises without Landlord's prior written consent and then only by contractors or mechanics approved by Landlord. All such work shall be done at such times and in such manner as Landlord may from time to time designate. All alterations, additions or improvements upon the premises, made by either party shall become the property of Landlord, and shall remain upon, and be surrendered with the premises at the termination of this lease. Any mechanic's lien filed against the premises, or the building, for work claimed to have been done for Tenant, shall be discharged by Tenant within ten days thereafter at Tenant's expenses by filing a bond as required by law.

    10. ASSIGNMENT & SUBLETTING. The Tenant shall not assign this Lease, or in any manner transfer any interest in the premises or sublet the premises or any part thereof, without the written consent of the

Landlord. In the event Tenant is a corporation, and control thereof changes at any time, landlord may declare such event a default under the lease.

11. USE. The premises shall be used only as _____ and shall not be used for any illegal purpose or in violation of any zoning laws or property restrictions. Tenant shall not keep or display any merchandise in any common areas without the written consent of the Landlord. Tenant shall maintain any display windows in neat and clear condition and shall not make any structural alterations to the premises without the written consent of the Landlord. Tenant agrees to at all times conduct his business in a reputable manner and to not hold any auctions, liquidations, fire, or bankruptcy sale without the written consent of the Landlord, which consent shall not unreasonably be withheld.

12. ENVIRONMENTAL LAWS. Tenant shall strictly comply with any and all local, state and federal environmental laws and regulations. In the event Tenant violates any such laws the Landlord may terminate this lease. Tenant shall remain liable for the cleanup of any such violation and for any other costs, fines or penalties based upon such violation.

13. LIABILITY. Landlord, its employees and agents shall not be liable for and Tenant will indemnify and save them harmless from, all fines, suits, claims, demands, losses and actions (including attorney's fees) for any injury to person or damage to, or loss of property on or about the premises, caused by the negligence or misconduct or breach of this lease by Tenant, its employees, subtenants, invitees, or by any other person entering the premises. Landlord shall not be liable for any loss or damages to any person or property occasioned by theft, fire, act of God, public emergency, injunction, riot, strike, war, insurrection, court order, requisitions of other governmental body or authority, by other Tenants of the building, their invitees, or by any other matter beyond control of Landlord, or from any cause whatever except Landlord's negligence. Tenant hereby acknowledges that Landlord has made no written or oral representations or warranties, either express or implied, as to any security measures or safeguards on or about the premises.

14. INSURANCE. Tenant shall keep in effect for the term of this lease a policy of liability insurance covering Tenant and Landlord against any liability arising out of any injury on or about the premises. The limit of said policy shall be $_____/$_____ for personal injury and $_____ for property damage. Landlord shall be a loss payee on said policy.

15. FIRE OR CASUALTY. In the event of a fire or other casualty to the premises: a) If the premises are not rendered untenantable in whole or in part, Landlord shall promptly, after receipt of insurance proceeds, repair the premises and the rent shall not abate; b) If the premises are rendered partially untenantable, Landlord shall promptly, after receipt of insurance proceeds, repair the premises, and the rent shall abate as to the untenantable part of the premises; c) If the premises are rendered totally untenantable, Landlord shall promptly, after receipt of insurance proceeds, rebuild the premises and the rent shall abate. If such occurs during the last two years of lease, Landlord may cancel this lease. The rent abatement shall not apply if Tenant has business interruption insurance. In the event that a mortgage holder requires that the insurance proceeds be used to retire the debt, then Landlord may cancel this lease.

16. ACCESS. Landlord reserves the right to enter the premises, upon giving reasonable notice, for the purpose of inspection, repair or showing to prospective tenants or purchasers.

17. LOCKS. If Tenant adds or changes locks on the premises, Landlord shall be given copies of the keys. Landlord shall at all times have keys for access to the premises.

18. PARKING AREAS. Tenant shall have the nonexclusive use of all parking areas about the premises. Parking areas are intended primarily for use by customers and Tenants shall not permit its employees to use such areas for the parking or storage of any automobiles, trucks or other vehicles except as may be approved and designated in writing by Landlord. The use of such parking areas shall at all times be subject to such reasonable rules and regulations as Landlord shall promulgate.

19. SIGNS & ADVERTISING. Tenant shall have the right to install and maintain at his own expense, a storefront sign subject to the written approval of the Landlord as to dimensions, location and design, which approval shall not be unreasonably withheld. Tenant agrees not to use any advertising media in the premises or common areas that shall be deemed objectionable to the Landlord or other Tenants such as loudspeakers, radio broadcasts or recorded music which can be heard outside the leased premises. Tenant shall not install any exterior awnings, banners or lighting without the written consent of the Landlord. Tenant shall not use the name of

the premises except as the address, or use any picture or likeness of the premises without the written consent of the Landlord.

20. FIXTURES. Any fixtures installed in the premises shall become the property of the Landlord and such fixtures may not be removed without the specific written consent of Landlord.

21. ABANDONMENT. In the event Tenant abandons the property prior to the expiration of the lease, Landlord may relet the premises and hold Tenant liable for any costs, lost rent or damage to the premises. Landlord may dispose of any personal property abandoned by Tenant.

22. DEFAULT/REMEDIES. In the event the Tenant fails to pay the rent, violates any of the terms of this lease, abandons the premises, transfers any interest in the premises by operation of law, in bankruptcy or by assignment to creditors, then Tenant shall be in default under this lease. Upon such default, Landlord may terminate this lease and retake possession for his own account, or may terminate this lease and retake possession for the account of the Tenant, holding the Tenant liable for any lost rent, or may let the unit sit vacant and declare the entire remaining balance of the rent immediately due and payable.

23. SURRENDER OF PREMISES. At the expiration of the term of this lease, Tenant shall immediately surrender possession of the premises in as good condition as at the start of this lease. The Tenant shall turn over to Landlord all keys to the premises, including keys made by Tenant or Tenant's agents.

24. SUBORDINATION. Tenant's interest in the premises shall be subordinate to any encumbrances now on or hereafter placed on the premises, to any advances made under such encumbrances, and to any extensions or renewals thereof. Tenant agrees to sign any documents indicating such subordination which may be required by lenders.

25. MECHANICS' LIENS. Tenant shall have no power or authority to create any lien or permit any lien to attach to the present estate, reversion or other estate of Landlord in the premises herein demised or on the building or other improvements thereon, and all material, men, contractors, artisans, mechanics and laborers and other persons contracting with Tenant with respect to the demised premises or any part thereof, are hereby charged with Notice that they must look to Tenant to secure payment of any bill for work done or material furnished or for any other purpose during the term of this lease. If any such lien attaches, or claim of lien is made, against the demised premises or the building of which said premises are a part, or on the land on which the building is erected and shall not be released by payment, bond or otherwise within thirty (30) days after notice thereof, the Landlord shall have the option of payment or discharging the same and Tenant agrees to reimburse Landlord promptly upon demand.

26. EMINENT DOMAIN. In the event any part of the premises is taken by eminent domain the Landlord shall be entitled to all damages awarded for diminution of the fee and leasehold. In the event that only part of the premises is taken and the remainder is still tenantable, the rent shall be prorated and the Tenant only liable for the portion of the premises still usable.

27. ENTIRE AGREEMENT. This lease constitutes the entire agreement between the parties and may not be modified except in writing signed by both parties.

28. WAIVER. One or more waivers of any covenant or condition by the Landlord shall not be construed as a waiver of a further breach of the same covenant or condition.

29. ATTORNEY'S FEES. In the event of any legal proceedings regarding this agreement, including appellate proceedings, the prevailing party shall be entitled to a reasonable attorney's fee. "Legal proceedings" shall include any legal services used prior to commencement of litigation.

30. JURY WAIVER. Both Landlord and Tenant hereby waive trial by jury in any action arising out of this agreement.

31. SEVERABILITY. If any provision of this lease should be or become invalid, such invalidity shall not in any way affect any of the other provisions of this lease which shall continue to remain in full force and effect.

32. RELATIONSHIP OF PARTIES. Nothing contained herein shall be deemed or construed by the parties hereto, nor by any third party, as creating the relationship of principal and agent or of partnership or of joint venture between the parties hereto, it being understood and agreed that neither the method of computation of rent nor any other provision contained herein, nor any acts of the parties herein, shall be deemed to create any relationship between the parties hereto other than the relationship of Landlord and Tenant.

33. NOTICES. Any notice given by the parties to this lease shall be served by certified mail at the following addresses or at such other addresses as provided in writing.

Landlord:_____

Tenant:_____

34. RECORDING. This lease shall not be recorded in any public records.

35. MISCELLANEOUS PROVISIONS. _____

_____.

WITNESS the hands and seals of the parties hereto this _____ day of _____, _____.

Witnesses: Landlord:

_____   _____

_____   _____

                                                        Tenant:

_____   _____

_____   _____

GUARANTEE. In consideration of the acceptance by Landlord of the above lease the undersigned jointly and severably guarantee full payment and performance of all obligations of Tenant under the lease.

_____

Guarantor

_____

Guarantor

COMMERCIAL LEASE—SHORT FORM

LANDLORD: _____   TENANT: _____

_____   _____

IN CONSIDERATION of the mutual covenants and conditions herein contained, Landlord leases to Tenant and Tenant leases from Landlord the property described under the following terms and conditions:

1. PREMISES. The premises consist of a _____ of approximately _____ square feet located at _____ together with the common use with other Tenants of all parking, roads and walkways and other public areas.

2. TERM. The term of this lease shall be for a period of _____ months commencing at 12:01 a.m. on _____, _____, and ending at midnight on _____, _____.

3. RENT. The base rent for the term of this lease shall be $_____ per month, together with any sales or use tax due for the rental of the premises.

4. PAYMENT. Payments must be received by Landlord on or before the due date at the following address:_____ or such place as designated by Landlord in writing. Tenant understands that this may require early mailing. In the event a check bounces, Landlord may require cash or certified funds.

5. SECURITY. Tenant shall pay to Landlord the sum of $_____ as last month's rent under this lease, plus $_____ as security deposit.

6. UTILITIES. The Tenant shall be responsible for all charges for electricity, gas, water, sewer or other utilities supplied to the premises. Any such charges not billed directly to Tenant shall be reimbursed to Landlord each month upon presentation of a statement.

7. MAINTENANCE & REPAIR. The Landlord shall keep the foundation, outer walls and roof of the premises and the common areas in good repair, except that Landlord shall not be liable for any repairs occasioned by the acts of Tenant, its agents or employees. Tenant shall be responsible for maintenance and repair to the inside of the premises including heating and cooling systems, electrical, plumbing, machinery, hardware, doors, windows, screens and painting. All such repairs shall be made with materials and workmanship equivalent to the original. Tenant shall be responsible for extermination service to the premises.

8. ALTERATIONS & IMPROVEMENTS. Tenant shall make no alterations or improvements to the premises (including paint) without the written consent of the Landlord and any such alterations or improvements shall become the property of the Landlord unless otherwise agreed to in writing.

9. ASSIGNMENT & SUBLETTING. The Tenant shall not assign this Lease, or in any manner transfer any interest in the premises or sublet the premises or any part thereof, without the written consent of the Landlord.

10. USE. The premises shall be used only as _____ and shall not be used for any illegal purpose or in violation of any zoning laws or property restrictions.

11. ENVIRONMENTAL LAWS. Tenant shall strictly comply with any and all local, state and federal environmental laws and regulations. In the event Tenant violates any such laws the Landlord may terminate this lease. Tenant shall remain liable for the cleanup of any such violation and for any other costs, fines or penalties based upon such violation.

12. PARKING AREAS. Tenant shall have the nonexclusive use of parking space for _____ cars. The use of such parking areas shall at all times be subject to such reasonable rules and regulations as Landlord shall promulgate.

13. LIABILITY. Tenant agrees to hold Landlord harmless from any and all claims for injuries or damages occurring on the premises, and to be solely responsible for insuring Tenant's own possessions on the premises.

14. INSURANCE. Tenant shall keep in effect for the term of this lease a policy of liability insurance covering Tenant and Landlord against any liability arising out of any injury on or about the premises. The limit of said policy shall be $_____/$_____ for personal injury and $_____ for property damage. Landlord shall be a loss payee on said policy.

15. FIRE OR CASUALTY. In the event the premises are partially damaged by fire or other casualty, Landlord shall repair same within ninety (90) days. In the event the premises are destroyed and untenantable the rent shall abate and Landlord may rebuild the premises within ninety (90) days or may cancel this lease.

16. ACCESS. Landlord reserves the right to enter the premises, for the purpose of inspection, repair or showing to prospective tenants or purchasers.

17. LOCKS. If Tenant adds or changes locks on the premises, Landlord shall be given copies of the keys. Landlord shall at all times have keys for access to the premises.

18. EMINENT DOMAIN. In the event any part of the premises is taken by eminent domain the Landlord shall be entitled to all damages awarded for diminution of the fee and leasehold and this lease shall terminate.

19. FIXTURES. Fixtures installed by Tenant on the premises shall remain the property of the Tenant provided the Tenant has not defaulted under this lease and provided that upon any such removal the premises shall be restored to their original condition. Lighting, plumbing, heating and air-conditioning equipment, whether or not installed by Tenant, shall not be removable but shall become the property of the Landlord.

20. ABANDONMENT. In the event Tenant abandons the property prior to the expiration of the lease, Landlord may relet the premises and hold Tenant liable for any costs, lost rent or damage to the premises. Landlord may dispose of any personal property abandoned by Tenant.

21. DEFAULT/REMEDIES. In the event the Tenant fails to pay the rent, violates any of the terms of this lease, abandons the premises, transfers any interest in the premises by operation of law, in bankruptcy or by assignment to creditors, then Tenant shall be in default under this lease. Upon such default, Landlord may terminate this lease and retake possession for his own account, or may terminate this lease and retake possession for the account of Tenant, holding Tenant liable for any lost rent, or may let the unit sit vacant and declare the entire remaining balance of the rent immediately due and payable.

22. SURRENDER OF PREMISES. At the expiration of the term of this lease, Tenant shall immediately surrender possession of the premises in as good condition as at the start of this lease. The Tenant shall turn over to Landlord all keys to the premises, including keys made by Tenant or Tenant's agents.

23. MECHANICS LIENS. The estate of Landlord shall not be subject to any liens for improvements contracted by Tenant.

24. ATTORNEY'S FEES. In the event Landlord must use the services of an attorney to enforce this agreement, Tenant shall pay Landlord's attorney fees.

25. SUBORDINATION. Tenant's interest in the premises shall be subordinate to any encumbrances now on or hereafter placed on the premises, to any advances made under such encumbrances, and to any extensions or renewals thereof. Tenant agrees to sign any documents indicating such subordination which may be required by lenders.

26. WAIVER. Any failure by Landlord to exercise any rights under this agreement shall not constitute a waiver of Landlord's rights.

27. SEVERABILITY. In the event any section of this agreement shall be held to be invalid, all remaining provisions shall remain in full force and effect.

28. RECORDING. This lease shall not be recorded in any public records.

29. MISCELLANEOUS PROVISIONS._____
_____
_____.

WITNESS the hands and seals of the parties hereto this _____ day of _____, _____.

Witnesses: Landlord:

_____   _____

_____   _____

                                                              Tenant:

_____   _____

_____   _____

GUARANTEE. In consideration of the acceptance by Landlord of the above lease the undersigned jointly and severably guarantee full payment and performance of all obligations of Tenant under the lease.

                                          _____
                                          Guarantor

                                          _____
                                          Guarantor

Storage Space Lease

Landlord:_____ Tenant: _____

_____   _____

Description of space leased:_____

IN CONSIDERATION of the mutual covenants and conditions herein contained, Landlord hereby leases to Tenant and Tenant leases from Landlord the above described property under the following terms and conditions:

    1. TERM. This lease shall begin on _____, _____, and end on _____, _____.

    2. RENT. The rent shall be $_____ per month and shall be due on or before the _____ day of each month. In the event the rent is received more than _____ days late, a late fee of $_____ shall be due. In the event a check bounces, a fee of $_____ shall be due.

    3. DEFAULT. In the event Tenant fails to pay the rent due under this agreement, Landlord may deny access until paid in full and whenever the rent is more than 30 days in arrears, Landlord may remove any property in the storage space and relet it to a new Tenant.

    4. LIEN. Landlord shall have a lien on any property placed in the storage space and shall have the right to sell the property at public or private sale or as provided by law.

    5. USE. Tenant shall not keep in the storage space any explosive, inflammable, hazardous or illegal substances or any animals or pets. Tenant shall not assign or sublet the storage space. Tenant shall abide by the rules and regulations of Landlord which are attached hereto. Landlord shall have the right to enter the storage space for inspection or repairs. Tenant shall make no alterations to the storage space without the written consent of Landlord.

    6. LIABILITY. This agreement is made on the express condition that, while Landlord shall exercise reasonable care in the operation of the premises, Landlord shall not be liable for any loss or damage to Tenant.

    7. CASUALTY. In the event the premises are damaged by fire or other casualty, and are rendered untenantable, either party may cancel this agreement.

    8. SECURITY DEPOSIT. Tenant shall deposit with Landlord the sum of $_____ to be returned upon the termination of this agreement provided Tenant is not in default hereof.

    9. TERMINATION. This agreement shall terminate as provided in paragraph 1. above unless renewed or extended in writing by both parties hereto.

    IN WITNESS WHEREOF, the parties have executed this lease the _____ day of _____, _____.

LANDLORD: TENANT:

_____   _____

This page intentionally left blank.

Storage Space Rental Agreement

Landlord:_____   Tenant: _____

_____   _____

Description of space leased:_____

IN CONSIDERATION of the mutual covenants and agreements herein contained, Landlord hereby leases to Tenant and Tenant hereby leases from Landlord the above described property under the following terms and conditions:

    1. TERM. This lease shall commence on _____, _____, and continue until terminated as provided herein.

    2. RENT. The rent shall be $_____ per month and shall be due on or before the _____ day of each month. In the event the rent is received more than _____ days late, a late fee of $_____ shall be due. In the event a check bounces, a fee of $_____ shall be due.

    3. DEFAULT. In the event Tenant fails to pay the rent due under this agreement, Landlord may deny access until paid in full and whenever the rent is more than 30 days in arrears, Landlord may remove any property in the storage space and relet it to a new Tenant.

    4. LIEN. Landlord shall have a lien on any property placed in the storage space and shall have the right to sell the property at public or private sale or as provided by law.

    5. USE. Tenant shall not keep in the storage space any explosive, inflammable, hazardous or illegal substances or any animals or pets. Tenant shall not assign or sublet the storage space. Tenant shall abide by the rules and regulations of Landlord which are attached hereto. Landlord shall have the right to enter the storage space for inspection or repairs. Tenant shall make no alterations to the storage space without the written consent of Landlord.

    6. LIABILITY. This agreement is made on the express condition that, while Landlord shall exercise reasonable care in the operation of the premises, Landlord shall not be liable for any loss or damage to Tenant.

    7. CASUALTY. In the event the premises are damaged by fire or other casualty, and are rendered untenantable, either party may cancel this Agreement.

    8. SECURITY DEPOSIT. Tenant shall deposit with Landlord the sum of $_____ to be returned upon the termination of this Agreement provided Tenant is not in default hereof.

    9. TERMINATION. This agreement may be terminated by either party upon the giving of written notice at least 30 days prior to the end of any rental month.

    IN WITNESS WHEREOF, the parties have executed this lease the _____ day of _____, _____.

LANDLORD: TENANT:

_____   _____

This page intentionally left blank.

SCHEDULE A

Inventory of Furnishings

APPLIANCES

___ Blender
___ Broiler
___ Can Opener
___ Clock Radio
___ Clocks
___ Clothes Dryer
___ Elec. Fry Pan
___ Floor Polisher
___ Garbage Disposal
___ Hair Dryer
___ Ice Crusher
___ Steam Iron
___ Ironing Board
___ Knife Sharpener
___ Mixer
___ Phonograph Equip.
___ Radios
___ Refrigerator
___ Rotisserie
___ Stove
___ Television
___ Toaster
___ Vacuum Cleaner
___ Waffle Iron
___ Washing Machine

CHINA & GLASSWARE

___ Bowls, Mixing
___ Bowls, Serving
___ Bowls, Soup
___ Coffeepots
___ Creamers
___ Cups
___ Dinner Plates
___ Egg Cups
___ Fruit Bowls
___ Glass Cooking Ware
___ Glasses
___ Platters
___ Pie Plates
___ Salad Plates
___ Salt/Pepper Shakers
___ Sauce Dishes
___ Saucers
___ Serving Dishes
___ Sugar Bowls
___ Teapots
___ Water Pitcher

FURNITURE & FURNISHINGS

___ Ashtrays
___ Beds, Single
___ Bed, Double
___ Carpets
___ Chairs, Armchair
___ Chairs, Dining
___ Chairs, Kitchen
___ Chest of Drawers
___ Consoles
___ Curtains, Bedroom
___ Curtains, Bathroom
___ Curtains, Kitchen
___ Desk
___ Drapes, Dining Rm.
___ Drapes, Living Rm.
___ Dressers
___ Lamps
___ Mattresses
___ Mirror, Walls
___ Pictures/Paintings
___ Shades/Blinds
___ Sofas
___ Tables, Coffee
___ Tables, Console
___ Tables, Dining
___ Tables, End
___ Tables, Kitchen
___ Tables, Misc.
___ Towel Racks
___ Vases
___ Waste Basket

KITCHEN UTENSILS

___ Baking Pans
___ Breadboards
___ Brooms
___ Buckets
___ Cake Pans
___ Canisters
___ Can Openers
___ Coffeepots
___ Colanders
___ Cooking Forks
___ Dish Drainer & Mat
___ Dish Pans
___ Double Boilers
___ Dust Pans
___ Egg Beaters
___ Flour Sieves
___ Frying Pans
___ Graters
___ Knives, Butcher
___ Knives, Other

___ Mixing Bowls
___ Mixing Spoons
___ Mops
___ Muffin Pans
___ Pie Plates
___ Potato Mashers
___ Roasters
___ Rolling Pins
___ Sauce Pans
___ Sink Strainer-s
___ Skillets
___ Soap Dishes
___ Tea Kettles
___ Trays

LINENS

___ Bath Mats
___ Bath Rugs
___ Bedspreads
___ Blankets, Double
___ Blankets, Single
___ Blankets, Electric
___ Mattress, Covers
___ Napkins
___ Pillow Slips
___ Sheets, Singles
___ Sheets, Double
___ Shower Curtains
___ Tablecloths
___ Towels, Bath
___ Towels, Hand
___ Washcloths

SILVERWARE

___ Butter Knives
___ Forks
___ Knives
___ Salad Forks
___ Soup Spoons
___ Sugar Spoons
___ Tablespoons
___ Teaspoons

MISCELLANEOUS

___ Electric Bulbs
    (state wattage)
___ Keys (describe)
___ Curtain Rods

List other items on reverse. All items in good condition unless noted otherwise.

This page intentionally left blank.

AMENDMENT TO LEASE/RENTAL AGREEMENT

The undersigned parties to that certain agreement dated _____,
_____ on the premises known as _____,
hereby agree to amend said agreement as follows:

WITNESS the hands and seals of the parties hereto this ____ day of _____,
_____.

Landlord: Tenant:

_____   _____

_____   _____

ASSIGNMENT OF LEASE

This Lease Assignment is entered into by and among _____
(the "Assignor"), _____ (the "Assignee"),
and _____ (the "Landlord").
For valuable consideration, it is agreed by the parties as follows:

1. The Landlord and the Assignor have entered into a lease agreement (the "Lease") dated _____, concerning the premises described as:

2. The Assignor hereby assigns and transfers to the Assignee all of Assignor's rights and delegates all of Assignor's duties under the Lease effective _____ (the "Effective Date").

3. The Assignee hereby accepts such assignment of rights and delegation of duties and agrees to pay all rents promptly when due and perform all of Assignor's obligations under the Lease accruing on and after the Effective Date. The Assignee further agrees to indemnify and hold the Assignor harmless from any breach of Assignee's duties hereunder.

4. ❑ The Assignor agrees to transfer possession of the leased premises to the Assignee on the Effective Date. All rents and obligations of the Assignor under the Lease accruing before the Effective Date shall have been paid or discharged.

   ❑ The Landlord hereby assents to the assignment of the Lease hereunder and as of the Effective Date hereby releases and discharges the Assignor from all duties and obligations under the Lease accruing after the Effective Date.

   ❑ The Landlord hereby assents to this lease assignment provided that the Landlord's assent shall not discharge the Assignor of any obligations under the Lease in the event of breach by the Assignee. The Landlord will give notice to the Assignor of any breach by the Assignee. If the Assignor pays all accrued rents and cures any other default of the Assignee, the Assignor may enforce the terms of the Lease and this Assignment against the Assignee, in the name of the Landlord, if necessary.

5. There shall be no further assignment of the Lease without the written consent of the Landlord.

6. This agreement shall be binding upon and inure to the benefit of the parties, their successors, assigns and personal representatives.

This assignment was executed under seal on _____.

Assignor: Assignee:

_____   _____

_____   _____

Landlord:

_____

_____

Disclosure of Information on Lead-Based Paint and/or Lead-Based Paint Hazards

Lead Warning Statement

Housing built before 1978 may contain lead-based paint. Lead from paint, paint chips, and dust can pose health hazards if not managed properly. Lead exposure is especially harmful to young children and pregnant women. Before renting pre-1978 housing, lessors must disclose the presence of known lead-based paint and/or lead-based paint hazards in the dwelling. Lessees must also receive a federally approved pamphlet on lead poisoning prevention.

Lessor's Disclosure

(a) Presence of lead-based paint and/or lead-based paint hazards (check (i) or (ii) below):

  (i) _____ Known lead-based paint and/or lead-based paint hazards are present in the housing (explain).

  _____

  _____

  (ii) _____ Lessor has no knowledge of lead-based paint and/or lead-based paint hazards in the housing.

(b) Records and reports available to the lessor (check (i) or (ii) below):

  (i) _____ Lessor has provided the lessee with all available records and reports pertaining to lead-based paint and/or lead-based paint hazards in the housing (list documents below).

  _____

  _____

  (ii) _____ Lessor has no reports or records pertaining to lead-based paint and/or lead-based paint hazards in the housing.

Lessee's Acknowledgment (initial)

(c) _____ Lessee has received copies of all information listed above.

(d) _____ Lessee has received the pamphlet *Protect Your Family from Lead in Your Home.*

Agent's Acknowledgment (initial)

(e) _____ Agent has informed the lessor of the lessor's obligations under 42 U.S.C. 4852(d) and is aware of his/her responsibility to ensure compliance.

Certification of Accuracy

The following parties have reviewed the information above and certify, to the best of their knowledge, that the information they have provided is true and accurate.

Lessor	Date	Lessor	Date
Lessee	Date	Lessee	Date
Agent	Date	Agent	Date

INDEX

Your #1 Source for Real World Legal Information...

SPHINX® PUBLISHING
An Imprint of Sourcebooks, Inc.®
- Written by lawyers
- Simple English explanation of the law
- Forms and instructions included

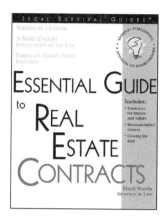

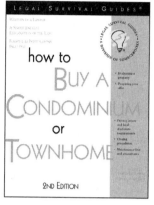

ESSENTIAL GUIDE TO REAL ESTATE CONTRACTS

This book makes it easy for people to develop their own contracts with clear explanation of the various clauses, their meanings, and uses. Includes easy-to-use, blank, tear-out forms and information about negotiating over the Internet.

192 pages; $18.95;
ISBN 1-57248-159-5

HOW TO BUY A CONDOMINIUM OR TOWNHOME, 2ND ED.

This new edition includes an updated appendix referencing each state's laws relating to condominiums and townhomes. Learn the difference between a single-family home, condominium, and/or cooperative, and a townhome in regards to ownership.

176 pages; $19.95;
ISBN 1-57248-164-1

See the following order form for books written specifically for California, Florida, Georgia, Illinois, Massachusetts, Michigan, Minnesota, New York, North Carolina, Ohio, Pennsylvania, and Texas!

What our customers say about our books:

"It couldn't be more clear for the lay person." —R.D.

"I want you to know I really appreciate your book. It has saved me a lot of time and money." —L.T.

"Your real estate contracts book has saved me nearly $12,000.00 in closing costs over the past year." —A.B.

"...many of the legal questions that I have had over the years were answered clearly and concisely through your plain English interpretation of the law." —C.E.H.

"If there weren't people out there like you I'd be lost. You have the best books of this type out there." —S.B.

"...your forms and directions are easy to follow." —C.V.M.

Sphinx Publishing's Legal Survival Guides
are directly available from the Sourcebooks, Inc., or from your local bookstores.
For credit card orders call 1–800–432–7444, write P.O. Box 4410, Naperville, IL 60567-4410,
or fax 630-961-2168

SPHINX® PUBLISHING'S NATIONAL TITLES

Valid in All 50 States

LEGAL SURVIVAL IN BUSINESS

How to Form a Delaware Corporation from Any State	$24.95
How to Form a Limited Liability Company	$22.95
Incorporate in Nevada from Any State	$24.95
How to Form a Nonprofit Corporation	$24.95
How to Form Your Own Corporation (3E)	$24.95
How to Form Your Own Partnership	$22.95
How to Register Your Own Copyright (3E)	$21.95
How to Register Your Own Trademark (3E)	$21.95
Most Valuable Business Legal Forms You'll Ever Need (2E)	$19.95
Most Valuable Corporate Forms You'll Ever Need (2E)	$24.95

LEGAL SURVIVAL IN COURT

Debtors' Rights (3E)	$14.95
Grandparents' Rights (3E)	$24.95
Help Your Lawyer Win Your Case (2E)	$14.95
Jurors' Rights (2E)	$12.95
Legal Research Made Easy (2E)	$16.95
Winning Your Personal Injury Claim (2E)	$24.95

LEGAL SURVIVAL IN REAL ESTATE

How to Buy a Condominium or Townhome	$19.95
How to Negotiate Real Estate Contracts (3E)	$18.95
How to Negotiate Real Estate Leases (3E)	$18.95

LEGAL SURVIVAL IN PERSONAL AFFAIRS

Cómo Hacer su Propio Testamento	$16.95
Guía de Inmigración a Estados Unidos (2E)	$24.95
Cómo Solicitar su Propio Divorcio	$24.95
How to File Your Own Bankruptcy (4E)	$21.95
How to File Your Own Divorce (4E)	$24.95
How to Make Your Own Will (2E)	$16.95
How to Write Your Own Living Will (2E)	$16.95
How to Write Your Own Premarital Agreement (2E)	$21.95
How to Win Your Unemployment Compensation Claim	$21.95
Living Trusts and Simple Ways to Avoid Probate (2E)	$22.95
Most Valuable Personal Legal Forms You'll Ever Need	$24.95
Neighbor v. Neighbor (2E)	$16.95
The Nanny and Domestic Help Legal Kit	$22.95
The Power of Attorney Handbook (3E)	$19.95
Repair Your Own Credit and Deal with Debt	$18.95
Social Security Benefits Handbook (2E)	$16.95
Unmarried Parents' Rights	$19.95
U.S.A. Immigration Guide (3E)	$19.95
Your Right to Child Custody, Visitation and Support	$22.95

Legal Survival Guides are directly available from Sourcebooks, Inc., or from your local bookstores.
Prices are subject to change without notice.

For credit card orders call 1–800–432–7444, write P.O. Box 4410, Naperville, IL 60567-4410
or fax 630-961-2168

SPHINX® PUBLISHING ORDER FORM

BILL TO:		SHIP TO:	
Phone #	Terms	F.O.B. Chicago, IL	Ship Date

Charge my: ☐ VISA   ☐ MasterCard   ☐ American Express

☐ **Money Order or Personal Check**

Credit Card Number   Expiration Date

Qty	ISBN	Title	Retail	Ext.	Qty	ISBN	Title	Retail	Ext.
		SPHINX PUBLISHING NATIONAL TITLES				1-57071-345-6	Most Valuable Bus. Legal Forms You'll Ever Need (2E)	$19.95	
	1-57248-148-X	Cómo Hacer su Propio Testamento	$16.95			1-57071-346-4	Most Valuable Corporate Forms You'll Ever Need (2E)	$24.95	
	1-57248-147-1	Cómo Solicitar su Propio Divorcio	$24.95			1-57248-130-7	Most Valuable Personal Legal Forms You'll Ever Need	$24.95	
	1-57071-342-1	Debtors' Rights (3E)	$14.95			1-57248-098-X	The Nanny and Domestic Help Legal Kit	$22.95	
	1-57248-139-0	Grandparents' Rights (3E)	$24.95			1-57248-089-0	Neighbor v. Neighbor (2E)	$16.95	
	1-57248-087-4	Guía de Inmigración a Estados Unidos (2E)	$24.95			1-57071-348-0	The Power of Attorney Handbook (3E)	$19.95	
	1-57248-103-X	Help Your Lawyer Win Your Case (2E)	$14.95			1-57248-149-8	Repair Your Own Credit and Deal with Debt	$18.95	
	1-57071-164-X	How to Buy a Condominium or Townhome	$19.95			1-57071-337-5	Social Security Benefits Handbook (2E)	$16.95	
	1-57071-223-9	How to File Your Own Bankruptcy (4E)	$21.95			1-57071-399-5	Unmarried Parents' Rights	$19.95	
	1-57248-132-3	How to File Your Own Divorce (4E)	$24.95			1-57071-354-5	U.S.A. Immigration Guide (3E)	$19.95	
	1-57248-100-5	How to Form a DE Corporation from Any State	$24.95			1-57248-138-2	Winning Your Personal Injury Claim (2E)	$24.95	
	1-57248-083-1	How to Form a Limited Liability Company	$22.95			1-57248-097-1	Your Right to Child Custody, Visitation and Support	$22.95	
	1-57248-099-8	How to Form a Nonprofit Corporation	$24.95				**CALIFORNIA TITLES**		
	1-57248-133-1	How to Form Your Own Corporation (3E)	$24.95			1-57248-150-1	CA Power of Attorney Handbook (2E)	$18.95	
	1-57071-343-X	How to Form Your Own Partnership	$22.95			1-57248-151-X	How to File for Divorce in CA (3E)	$26.95	
	1-57248-119-6	How to Make Your Own Will (2E)	$16.95			1-57071-356-1	How to Make a CA Will	$16.95	
	1-57071-331-6	How to Negotiate Real Estate Contracts (3E)	$18.95			1-57248-145-5	How to Probate and Settle an Estate in California	$26.95	
	1-57071-332-4	How to Negotiate Real Estate Leases (3E)	$18.95			1-57248-146-3	How to Start a Business in CA	$18.95	
	1-57248-124-2	How to Register Your Own Copyright (3E)	$21.95			1-57071-358-8	How to Win in Small Claims Court in CA	$16.95	
	1-57248-104-8	How to Register Your Own Trademark (3E)	$21.95			1-57071-359-6	Landlords' Rights and Duties in CA	$21.95	
	1-57071-349-9	How to Win Your Unemployment Compensation Claim	$21.95				**FLORIDA TITLES**		
	1-57248-118-8	How to Write Your Own Living Will (2E)	$16.95			1-57071-363-4	Florida Power of Attorney Handbook (2E)	$16.95	
	1-57071-344-8	How to Write Your Own Premarital Agreement (2E)	$21.95			1-57248-093-9	How to File for Divorce in FL (6E)	$24.95	
	1-57248-158-7	Incorporate in Nevada from Any State	$24.95			1-57071-380-4	How to Form a Corporation in FL (4E)	$24.95	
	1-57071-333-2	Jurors' Rights (2E)	$12.95			1-57248-086-6	How to Form a Limited Liability Co. in FL	$22.95	
	1-57071-400-2	Legal Research Made Easy (2E)	$16.95			1-57071-401-0	How to Form a Partnership in FL	$22.95	
	1-57071-336-7	Living Trusts and Simple Ways to Avoid Probate (2E)	$22.95			1-57248-113-7	How to Make a FL Will (6E)	$16.95	

Form Continued on Following Page   **SUBTOTAL**

To order, call Sourcebooks at 1-800-432-7444 or FAX (630) 961-2168 (Bookstores, libraries, wholesalers—please call for discount)

Prices are subject to change without notice.

SPHINX® PUBLISHING ORDER FORM

Qty	ISBN	Title	Retail	Ext.
____	1-57248-088-2	How to Modify Your FL Divorce Judgment (4E)	$24.95	____
____	1-57248-144-7	How to Probate and Settle and Estate in FL (4E)	$26.95	____
____	1-57248-081-5	How to Start a Business in FL (5E)	$16.95	____
____	1-57071-362-6	How to Win in Small Claims Court in FL (6E)	$16.95	____
____	1-57248-123-4	Landlords' Rights and Duties in FL (8E)	$21.95	____
		GEORGIA TITLES		
____	1-57248-137-4	How to File for Divorce in GA (4E)	$21.95	____
____	1-57248-075-0	How to Make a GA Will (3E)	$16.95	____
____	1-57248-140-4	How to Start a Business in Georgia (2E)	$16.95	____
		ILLINOIS TITLES		
____	1-57071-405-3	How to File for Divorce in IL (2E)	$21.95	____
____	1-57071-415-0	How to Make an IL Will (2E)	$16.95	____
____	1-57071-416-9	How to Start a Business in IL (2E)	$18.95	____
____	1-57248-078-5	Landlords' Rights & Duties in IL	$21.95	____
		MASSACHUSETTS TITLES		
____	1-57248-128-5	How to File for Divorce in MA (3E)	$24.95	____
____	1-57248-115-3	How to Form a Corporation in MA	$24.95	____
____	1-57248-108-0	How to Make a MA Will (2E)	$16.95	____
____	1-57248-106-4	How to Start a Business in MA (2E)	$18.95	____
____	1-57248-107-2	Landlords' Rights and Duties in MA (2E)	$21.95	____
		MICHIGAN TITLES		
____	1-57071-409-6	How to File for Divorce in MI (2E)	$21.95	____
____	1-57248-077-7	How to Make a MI Will (2E)	$16.95	____
____	1-57071-407-X	How to Start a Business in MI (2E)	$16.95	____
		MINNESOTA TITLES		
____	1-57248-142-0	How to File for Divorce in MN	$21.95	____
		NEW YORK TITLES		
____	1-57248-141-2	How to File for Divorce in NY (2E)	$26.95	____
____	1-57248-105-6	How to Form a Corporation in NY	$24.95	____
____	1-57248-095-5	How to Make a NY Will (2E)	$16.95	____
____	1-57071-185-2	How to Start a Business in NY	$18.95	____
____	1-57071-187-9	How to Win in Small Claims Court in NY	$16.95	____

Qty	ISBN	Title	Retail	Ext.
____	1-57071-186-0	Landlords' Rights and Duties in NY	$21.95	____
____	1-57071-188-7	New York Power of Attorney Handbook	$19.95	____
____	1-57248-122-6	Tenants' Rights in NY	$21..95	____
		NORTH CAROLINA TITLES		
____	1-57071-326-X	How to File for Divorce in NC (2E)	$22.95	____
____	1-57248-129-3	How to Make a NC Will (3E)	$16.95	____
____	1-57248-096-3	How to Start a Business in NC (2E)	$16.95	____
____	1-57248-091-2	Landlords' Rights & Duties in NC	$21.95	____
		OHIO TITLES		
____	1-57248-190-0	How to File for Divorce in OH (2E)	$24.95	____
		PENNSYLVANIA TITLES		
____	1-57248-127-7	How to File for Divorce in PA (2E)	$24.95	____
____	1-57248-094-7	How to Make a PA Will (2E)	$16.95	____
____	1-57248-112-9	How to Start a Business in PA (2E)	$18.95	____
____	1-57071-179-8	Landlords' Rights and Duties in PA	$19.95	____
		TEXAS TITLES		
____	1-57071-330-8	How to File for Divorce in TX (2E)	$21.95	____
____	1-57248-114-5	How to Form a Corporation in TX (2E)	$24.95	____
____	1-57071-417-7	How to Make a TX Will (2E)	$16.95	____
____	1-57071-418-5	How to Probate an Estate in TX (2E)	$22.95	____
____	1-57071-365-0	How to Start a Business in TX (2E)	$18.95	____
____	1-57248-111-0	How to Win in Small Claims Court in TX (2E)	$16.95	____
____	1-57248-110-2	Landlords' Rights and Duties in TX (2E)	$21.95	____

SUBTOTAL THIS PAGE ____

SUBTOTAL PREVIOUS PAGE ____

Shipping— $5.00 for 1st book, $1.00 each additional ____

Illinois residents add 6.75% sales tax ____

Connecticut residents add 6.00% sales tax ____

TOTAL ____

To order, call Sourcebooks at 1-800-432-7444 or FAX (630) 961-2168 (Bookstores, libraries, wholesalers—please call for discount)
Prices are subject to change without notice.